ONE HUNDRED LAMPS FOR THE SOUL

Also by Celia Haddon

One Hundred Secret Thoughts Cats Have About Humans
One Hundred Ways for a Cat to Find Its Inner Kitten
One Hundred Ways for a Cat to Train Its Human
One Hundred Ways to a Happy Cat
One Hundred Ways to Be Happy
One Hundred Ways to Comfort
One Hundred Ways to Friendship
One Hundred Ways to Say I Love You
One Hundred Ways to Say Thank You
One Hundred Ways to Serenity

ONE HUNDRED LAMPS FOR THE SOUL

COMPILED BY

CELIA HADDON

Hodder & Stoughton
LONDON SYDNEY AUCKLAND

First published in Great Britain in 2003
This paperback edition first published in 2004

10 9 8 7 6 5 4 3 2 1

British Library Cataloguing in Publication Data
A record for this book is available from the British Library

ISBN 0 340 78599 3

Printed and bound in Great Britain by
Clays Ltd, St Ives plc

Hodder & Stoughton
A Division of Hodder Headline Ltd
338 Euston Road
London NW1 3BH
www.madaboutbooks.com

CONTENTS

ACKNOWLEDGMENTS

I have tried my best to obtain permission from copyright holders to reproduce the quotations in this book, but there are some I could not trace. The publishers will be happy to rectify any omissions in future editions.

I should like to thank the following for permission to reprint extracts:

Alcoholics Anonymous. The Twelve Steps are reprinted with permission of Alcoholics Anonymous World Services, Inc. (A.A.W.S.). Permission to reprint the Twelve Steps does not mean that A.A.W.S. has reviewed or approved the contents of this publication, or that A.A.W.S. necessarily agrees with the views expressed herein. A.A. is a program of recovery from alcoholism *only* – use of the Twelve Steps in connection with programs and activities which are patterned after A.A., but which address other problems, or in any other non-A.A. context, does not imply otherwise.

Robert L. Bell for permission to reprint 'Desiderata' by Max Ehrmann, © 1927 by Max Ehrmann. Reprinted by permission of Robert L. Bell, 427 South Shore Drive, Sarasota, Florida 34234, USA.

Dr Sheila Cassidy for permission to quote a passage, exact source unknown.

Columbia University Press for permission to quote from *Essays in Idleness: The Tsurezuregusa of Kenko*, translated by Donald Keene. © 1998 Columbia University Press. Reprinted with permission from the publisher.

Darton, Longman & Todd for an extract taken from *Beasts and Saints*, translated by Helen Waddell and edited by Esther de Waal, published and copyright © 1995 by Darton, Longman & Todd Ltd, and used by permission of the publishers.

Editions du Seuil, Paris, France, for an extract from *Le Divin Milieu* by Pierre Teilhard de Chardin, © Editions du Seuil, 1957.

Janet Farrar and Gavin Bone of Wicca and R. Cooke (on behalf of the late Doreen Valiente) for permission to use an extract from the pagan charge found in *Eight Sabbats for Witches* and *Rites for Birth, Marriage and Death*, by Janet and Stewart Farrar, published by Robert Hale, 1992.

The Revd Matthew Fox of the University of Creation Spirituality, 2141, Broadway, Oakland, CA 94612, USA (www.creationspirituality.org) for permission to quote an extract from *Original Blessing* by Matthew Fox, copyright © 1983 by Bear & Company, Inc. *See also* Penguin Putnam, Inc.

HarperCollins Publishers, Inc for an extract from pages 34–7 (edited) of *The Divin Milieu* by Pierre Teilhard de Chardin. Copyright © 1957 by Editions du Seuil, Paris. English translation copyright © 1960 by Wm. Collins Sons & Co., London, and Harper & Row, Publishers, Inc., New York. Renewed © 1988 by Harper & Row Publishers, Inc. Reprinted by permission of HarperCollins Publishers, Inc.

Maharishi Foundation for help in trying to trace a quotation from a talk by His Divinity Swami Brahmanda Saraswati. In lieu of finding a copyright holder, I have made a donation to the Foundation.

The Nilgiri Press for extracts from the 'Bhagavad-Gita', translated by Eknath Easwaran, founder of the Blue Mountain Center of Meditation, copyright © 1985; reprinted by permission of Nilgiri Press, Tomales, California, www.nilgiri.org.

The Open Church Foundation (PO Box 81389-0004, Wellesley Hills, MA 02181, USA) for 'Slow Me Down, Lord' by Orin L. Crain.

Open Court Publishing for extracts from 'The Gospel of Buddha', arranged by Paul Carus, 1894, which are by courtesy of The Open Court Publishing Company, Peru, Illinois, USA.

Oxford University Press for an extract from A *Confession and the Gospel in* Brief by Leo Tolstoy, translated by Aylmer Maude, with an introduction by the Hon. Mrs Alfred Lyttelton, The Tolstoy Centenary Edition for the Tolstoy Society, 1933. Reprinted by permission of Oxford University Press.

The Penguin Group (UK) for permission to quote 47 verses from the 'Bhagavad-Gita', translated by Eknath Easwaran, with chapter introductions by Diana Morrison (Arkana, 1986). Copyright © The Blue Mountain Center for Meditation, 1985.

The Penguin Group (UK) for permission to quote a passage from *The Koran*, translated by N.J. Dawood (Penguin Classics 1956, Fifth revised edition 1990). Copyright © N.J. Dawood, 1956, 1959, 1966, 1968, 1974, 1990.

Penguin Putnam, Inc for a passage from *Original Blessing* by Matthew Fox, copyright © 1983 by Bear & Company, Inc. Used by permission of Jeremy P. Tarcher, a division of Penguin Putnam, Inc.

SCM-Canterbury Press, for an extract from *Honest to God* by John A. T. Robinson, SCM Press, 1963. Also Westminster John Knox Press. The extract is reproduced from *Honest to God* by J.A.T. Robinson. Copyright ©1963 by SCM Press, Ltd. Used by permission of Westminster John Knox Press.

SCM-Canterbury Press for 'Morning Prayers' from 'Prayers for Fellow Prisoners' in *Letters and Papers from Prison* by Dietrich Bonhoeffer, The Enlarged Edition, SCM Press, 1971. Also

Simon & Schuster, Inc. for 'Prayer for Fellow Prisoners, Christmas 1943 – Morning Prayers'. This extract is reprinted with the permission of Scribner, an imprint of Simon and Schuster Adult Publishing Group, from *Letters and Papers from Prison*, Revised, Enlarged Edition, by Dietrich Bonhoeffer. Copyright © 1953, 1967, 1971 by SCM Press Ltd.

SCM-Canterbury Press for an extract from *The Shaking of the Foundations* by Paul Tillich, SCM Press, 1949. This extract is also reprinted with the permission of Scribner, an imprint of Simon & Schuster Adult Publishing Group, from the *The Shaking of the Foundations* by Paul Tillich. Copyright © 1948 by Charles Scribner's Sons; copyright renewed © 1976 by Hannah Tillich.

Simon & Schuster for the prayer 'Surrender', reprinted with the permission of Simon & Schuster from *Every Day I Pray* by Iyania Vanzant. Copyright © 2001 Inner Visions Worldwide Network, Inc.

Toc H for for help in trying to trace Oliver Warner whose prayer appeared in *Yours Is the Glory*, published 1971 by Toc H. In lieu of finding a copyright holder I have made a donation to Toc H.

United Synagogue Publications for extracts from The Authorised Daily Prayer Book of the United Hebrew Congregations of the Commonwealth, original translation by the Rev. S. Singer, enlarged under the Authority of the Chief Rabbi, Dr Jonathan Sacks, 1998, © Singer's Prayer Book Publication Committee, 1992.

The Arthur Waley Estate for extracts from passages from *Tao Te Ching* and a passage by Mencius from *The Way and Its Power*, by Arthur Waley, George Allen and Unwin, 1934

INTRODUCTION

Choosing a hundred spiritual passages is, in a way, an impossible task. So I have chosen the spiritual passages which have been a light for me – have comforted me, made me think, made me try harder to change my life, and sometimes, in the darkest hours of all, stopped me from falling into utter despair. In the end it has to be a personal choice.

Other people would have made other choices. Some of the great spiritual classics are missing from this book – because I haven't read them, or because they were not important to me. They didn't speak to my heart.

I have chosen passages which were inspiring to me as I journeyed through life. And I hope that at least some of them will be of interest even to those who do not follow a religion – agnostics, even atheists. I have tried to choose spiritual rather than religious passages. I made a decision that this would not be a specifically Christian anthology.

Some of the passages come from faiths which are relatively strange to me, a Christian. That very strangeness has helped me, throwing a light upon an old problem or making me think afresh. Different faiths can, I hope, learn from each other. Sometimes the familiar message, so familiar that I do not pay attention to it, gets through to me by a different spiritual tradition.

Some of the pieces of text were given to me by friends, often photocopied from one person to another, without an author's name. They were passed on because others had found them helpful. They are not always well written, but what they say has been important to me. Often I do not know where they originally came from.

Others are wonderfully written. Each time I read the writings of Thomas Traherne, for instance, I feel the shiver of pleasure that beautiful prose gives, as well as the inspiration of the way he looks at life. He is probably my favourite writer in this selection, and I hope that those who have not read him before will look up more of his writings.

Indeed there are many passages in this book that are only a taste of a remarkable book. Classics like John Bunyan's *Pilgrim's Progress* or modern books like Matthew Fox's *Original Blessing* will repay reading in full.

Some texts, like the Lord's Prayer or Psalm 23 are very familiar. Others, like the writing of Jacob Bauthumley, are (as I think) spiritual masterpieces which have been inexplicably neglected. Other passages, like those from William Blake, or from the *Tao Te Ching*, or the first chapter of St John's Gospel, I am not sure if I even understand properly. Yet in reading them I find something more than the mere words or perhaps I understand, as the *Tao Te Ching* might put it, something in the empty space between the words.

The passages are not placed in order of time, or of greatness, or even in order of their importance to me personally. Some passages from the New Testament, which do matter a great deal to me, I have left out because they have too much Christian theology to be easily acceptable to non-

Christians or to those Christians who feel unresolved anger against their Church.

The story of how God came into a moment of history – born as a baby to a modest craftsman's family, in a stable manger not a house, taking his first breaths among the hard-worked donkeys and oxen – is not in this book. It moves me greatly. But I felt it was too specifically Christian. I should have excluded the first chapter of St John's Gospel on the same criterion but I just could not bear to leave it out.

Because they have to be placed in some kind of order, I have put the passages into themes. There are some notes about some of the passages at the end of the book. Where it is necessary for full understanding, I have put a few introductory words before a passage.

These are the passages which are lamps for my soul.

CHAPTER ONE

THE HOLINESS OF CREATION AND CREATURES

I BEGIN WITH THE GREAT SPIRITUAL passages about the wonder and beauty of creation. If I want to lead a spiritual life, I can open my eyes to the beauty and wonder of the world and be grateful for them. This change in attitude requires no theological belief at all. Even a committed atheist can see the wonders of the universe, of the earth and its creatures. We live in a place of commonplace magic – from the wheeling stars and planets of the night sky to the tiny creatures in the grass. For me it is the place to start.

I

YOUR ENJOYMENT OF THE WORLD ...

Your enjoyment of the world is never right, till you so esteem it, that everything in it, is more your treasure than a king's exchequer full of gold and silver. And that exchequer yours also in place and service. Can you take too much joy in your Father's works? He is Himself in everything. Some things are little on the outside, and rough and common, but I remember the time when the dusts of the streets were as pleasing as gold to my infant eyes, and now they are more precious to the eye of reason ...

You never enjoy the world aright, till you see how a sand exhibiteth the wisdom and power of God: and prize in everything the service which they do you, by manifesting His glory and goodness to your soul, far more than the visible beauty on their surface or the material services they can do your body. Wine by its moisture quencheth my thirst, whether I consider it or no: but to see it flowing from His love who gave it unto man, quencheth the thirst even of the holy angels. To consider it, is to drink it spiritually. To rejoice in its diffusion is to be of a public mind. And to take pleasure in all the benefits it doth to all is heavenly, for so they do in heaven. To do so, is to be divine and good, and to imitate our infinite and eternal Father.

Your enjoyment of the world is never right, till every morning you awake in heaven; see yourself in your Father's palace; and look upon the skies, the earth, and the air as celestial joys: having such a reverend esteem of all, as if you were among the angels. The bride of a monarch, in her husband's chamber, hath no such causes of delight as you.

You never enjoy the world aright, till the sea itself floweth in your veins, till you are clothed with the heavens, and crowned with the stars: and perceive yourself to be the sole heir of the whole world, and more than so, because men are in it who are every one sole heirs as well as you. Till you can sing and rejoice and delight in God, as misers do in gold, and kings in sceptres, you never enjoy the world.

Till your spirit filleth the whole world, and the stars are your jewels; till you are as familiar with the ways of God in all ages as with your walk and table: till you are intimately acquainted with that shady nothing out of which the world was made; till you love men so as to desire their happiness, with a thirst equal to the zeal of your own: till you delight in God for being good to all; you never enjoy the world. Till you more feel it than your private estate, and are more present in the hemisphere, considering the glories and the beauties there, than in your own house; till you remember how lately you were made, and how wonderful it was when you came into it: and the more rejoice in the palace of your glory, than if it had been made but today morning.

Yet further, you never enjoy the world aright, till you so love the beauty of enjoying it, that you are covetous and earnest to persuade others to enjoy it. And so perfectly hate the abominable corruption of men in despising it, that you had rather suffer the flames of hell than willingly be guilty of their error. There is so much blindness and ingratitude and damned folly in it. The world is a mirror of infinite beauty, yet no man sees it. It is a temple of majesty, yet no man regards it. It is a region of light and peace, did not men disquiet it. It is the paradise of God. It is more to man since he is fallen than it was before. It is the place of angels and the gate of heaven …

From *Centuries of Meditations* by Thomas Traherne, seventeenth century

2

THE BEGINNING OF CREATION

In the beginning
God created the heaven and the earth.
And the earth was without form, and void; and darkness was upon the face of the deep. And the Spirit of God moved upon the face of the waters.
And God said, Let there be light: and there was light.
And God saw the light, that it was good: and God divided the light from the darkness.
And God called the light Day, and the darkness he called Night. And the evening and the morning were the first day.

And God said, Let there be a firmament in the midst of the waters, and let it divide the waters from the waters.

And God made the firmament, and divided the waters which were under the firmament from the waters which were above the firmament: and it was so.

And God called the firmament Heaven. And the evening and the morning were the second day.

And God said, Let the waters under the heaven be gathered together unto one place, and let the dry land appear: and it was so.

And God called the dry land Earth; and the gathering together of the waters called he Seas: and God saw that it was good.

And God said, Let the earth bring forth grass, the herb yielding seed, and the fruit tree yielding fruit after his kind, whose seed is in itself, upon the earth: and it was so.

And the earth brought forth grass, and herb yielding seed after his kind, and the tree yielding fruit, whose seed was in itself, after his kind: and God saw that it was good.

And the evening and the morning were the third day.

And God said, Let there be lights in the firmament of the heaven to divide the day from the night; and let them be for signs, and for seasons, and for days, and years:

And let them be for lights in the firmament of the heaven to give light upon the earth: and it was so.

And God made two great lights; the greater light to rule the day, and the lesser light to rule the night: he made the stars also.

And God set them in the firmament of the heaven to give light upon the earth,

And to rule over the day and over the night, and to divide the light from the darkness: and God saw that it was good.

And the evening and the morning were the fourth day.

And God said, Let the waters bring forth abundantly the moving creature that hath life, and fowl that may fly above the earth in the open firmament of heaven.

And God created great whales, and every living creature that moveth, which the waters brought forth abundantly, after their kind, and every winged fowl after his kind: and God saw that it was good.

And God blessed them, saying, Be fruitful, and multiply, and fill the waters in the seas, and let fowl multiply in the earth.

And the evening and the morning were the fifth day.

And God said, Let the earth bring forth the living creature after his kind, cattle, and creeping thing, and beast of the earth after his kind: and it was so.

And God made the beast of the earth after his kind, and cattle after their kind, and every thing that creepeth upon the earth after his kind: and God saw that it was good.

Genesis 1:1–25

3

LIGHT

In the name of God, the Compassionate, the Merciful …

Do you not see how God is praised by those in the heavens and those on earth? The very birds praise Him as they wing their way. He notes the prayers and praises of all His creatures; God has knowledge of all their actions.

It is God who has sovereignty over the heavens and the earth. To God shall all return.

Do you not see how God drives the clouds, then gathers and piles them up in masses which pour down torrents of rain? From heaven's mountains He sends down the hail, pelting with it whom He will and turning it away from whom He pleases. The flash of his lightning almost snatches out men's eyes.

God makes the night succeed the day; surely in this there is a lesson for clear-sighted men.

God created every beast from water. Some creep upon their bellies, others walk on two legs, and others yet on four. God creates what he pleases. God has power over all things.

'Light', The Koran 24, 41–5

4

GOD IN THE WORLD

O God Beautiful, O God Beautiful!!
In the forest you are Green
In the mountains you are High
In the river you are Restless
In the ocean you are Grave
To the servant you are Service
To the lover you are Love
To the sorrowful you are Sympathy
To the yogi you are Bliss
O God Beautiful, O God Beautiful
At Thy feet, O do I bow!!

Guru Nanak, founder of Sikhism,
sixteenth century

5

SEEING THE WORLD

And I know that this world is a world of imagination and vision. I see every thing I paint in this world but everybody does not see alike. To the eyes of a miser a guinea is far more beautiful than the sun, and a bag worn with the use of money has more beautiful proportions than a vine filled with grapes. The tree which moves some to tears of joy is in the eyes of others only a green thing which stands in the way. Some see nature all ridicule and deformity, and by these I shall not regulate my proportions; and some scarce see nature at all. But to the eyes of the man of imagination, nature is imagination itself. As a man is, so he sees. As the eye is formed, such are its powers …

'When the sun rises, do you not see a round disk of fire, somewhat like a guinea?' O no, no, I see an innumerable company of the heavenly host crying 'Holy, holy, holy is the Lord God Almighty.' I question not my corporeal or vegetative eye any more than I would question a window concerning a sight. I look through it and not with it …

If the doors or perception were cleansed every thing would appear to man as it is, infinite.

For man has closed himself up, till he sees all things through narrow chinks of his cavern …

How do you know but every bird that cuts the airy way, is an immense world of delight, closed by your senses five? …

For every thing that lives is Holy.

From the letters and notes of William Blake, nineteenth century

6

CHERRY BLOSSOM AND TRANSIENCE

Are we to look at cherry blossoms only in full bloom, the moon only when it is cloudless? To long for the moon while looking on the rain, to lower the blinds and be unaware of the passing of the spring – these are even more deeply moving. Branches about to blossom or gardens strewn with faded flowers are worthier of our admiration. Are poems written on such themes as 'Going to view the cherry blossoms only to find they had scattered' or 'On being prevented from visiting the blossom' inferior to those on 'Seeing the blossoms'? People commonly regret that the cherry blossoms scatter or that the moon sinks in the sky, and this is natural; but only an exceptionally insensitive man would say, 'This branch and that branch have lost their blossoms. There is nothing worth seeing now.'

In all things, it is the beginnings and ends that are

interesting. Does the love between men and women refer only to the moments when they are in each other's arms? The man who grieves over a love affair broken off before it was fulfilled, who bewails empty vows, who spends long autumn nights alone, who lets his thoughts wander to distant skies, who yearns for the past in a dilapidated house – such a man truly knows what love means.

The moon that appears close to dawn after we have long waited for it moves us more profoundly than the full moon shining cloudless over a thousand leagues. And how incomparably lovely is the moon, almost greenish in its light, when seen through the tops of the cedars deep in the mountains, or when it hides for a moment behind clustering clouds during a sudden shower! The sparkle on hickory or white-oak leaves seemingly wet with moonlight strikes one to the heart. One suddenly misses the capital, longing for a friend who could share the moment.

And are we to look at the moon and the cherry blossoms with our eyes alone? How much more evocative and pleasing it is to think about the spring without stirring from the house, to dream of the moonlit night though we remain in our room!

The man of breeding never appears to abandon himself completely to his pleasures; even his manner of enjoyment is detached. It is the rustic boors who take all their pleasures grossly. They squirm their way through the crowd to get under the trees; they stare at the blossoms with eyes for nothing else; they drink saké and compose linked verse; and finally they heartlessly break off great branches and cart them away.

When they see a spring they dip their hands and feet to cool them; if it is the snow, they jump down to leave their footprints. No matter what the sight, they are never content merely with looking at it …

It is charming on the day of the Festival to see garlands of hollyhock leaves carelessly strewn over everything. The morning of the Festival, before dawn breaks, you wonder who the owners are of the carriages silently drawn up in place, and guess, 'That one is his – or his,' and have your guesses confirmed when sometimes you recognise a coachman or servant. I never weary of watching the different carriages going back and forth, some delightfully unpretentious, others magnificent. By the time it is growing dark you wonder where the rows of carriages and the dense crowds of spectators have disappeared to. Before you know it, hardly a soul is left, and the congestion of returning carriages is over. Then they start removing the blinds and matting from the stands, and the place, even as you watch, begins to look desolate. You realise with a pang of grief that life is like this. If you have seen the avenues of the city, you have seen the festival.

I suddenly realised, from the large number of people I could recognise in the crowds passing to and fro before the stands, that there were not so many people in the world after all. Even if I were not to die until all of them had gone, I should not have long to wait. If you pierce a tiny aperture in a large vessel filled with water, even though only a small amount drips out, the constant leakage will empty the vessel. In this capital, with all its many people, surely a day never passes without someone dying … It does not matter how young or how strong you may be, the hour of death comes sooner than you expect. It is an extraordinary miracle that you should have escaped to this day; do you suppose you have even the briefest respite in which to relax?

From 'The Tusrezuregusa of Kenko,' fourteenth century.

7

BLESSINGS ON VARIOUS OCCASIONS

On eating fruit which grows on trees:

Blessed are You – the Lord our God, King of the universe, who creates the fruit of the tree.

On eating fruit which grows on the ground, vegetables, etc.:

Blessed are You – the Lord our God, King of the universe, who creates the fruit of the earth.

On partaking of flesh, fish, eggs, cheese, etc., or drinking any liquor except Wine:

Blessed are You – the Lord our God, King of the universe, by whose word all things exist.

On smelling fragrant woods or barks:

Blessed are You – the Lord our God, King of the universe, who creates fragrant woods.

On smelling fragrant plants:

Blessed are You – the Lord our God, King of the universe, who creates fragrant plants.

On smelling fragrant fruits:

Blessed are You – the Lord our God, King of the universe, who gives a goodly scent to fruits.

On smelling fragrant spices:

Blessed are You – the Lord our God, King of the universe, who creates various kinds of spices.

On smelling fragrant oils:

Blessed are You – the Lord our God, King of the universe, who creates fragrant oil.

On seeing lightning, shooting stars, high mountains, or vast deserts:

Blessed are You – the Lord our God, King of the universe, who performs the work of creation.

On hearing thunder:

Blessed are You – the Lord our God, King of the universe, whose might and power fill the world.

On seeing the ocean:

Blessed are You – the Lord our God, King of the universe, who has made the great sea.

On seeing beautiful trees or animals:

Blessed are You – the Lord our God, King of the universe, who has such as these in His world.

On seeing the rainbow:

Blessed are You – the Lord our God, King of the universe, who remembers the covenant, is faithful to His covenant, and keeps His promise.

From *The Jewish Authorised Daily Prayer Book*, current edition

8

THE SPIRITUALITY OF THE LAND TO NATIVE AMERICANS

To us the ashes of our ancestors are sacred and their resting place is hallowed ground. You wander far from the graves of your ancestors and seemingly without regret. Your religion was written on tablets of stone by the iron finger of your God so that you could not forget. The Red Man could never comprehend or remember it. Our religion is the traditions of our ancestors – the dreams of our old men, given them in solemn hours of the night by the Great Spirit; and visions of our sachems, and is written in the hearts of our people.

Your dead cease to love you and the land of their nativity as soon as they pass the portals of the tomb and wander away beyond the stars. They are soon forgotten and never return. Our dead never forget this beautiful world that gave them being. They still love its verdant valleys, its murmuring rivers, its magnificent mountains, sequestered vales and verdant lined lakes and bays, and ever yearn in tender fond affection over the lonely hearted living, and often return from the happy hunting ground to visit, guide, console, and comfort them.

Day and night cannot dwell together. The Red Man has ever fled the approach of the White Man, as the morning mist flees before the morning sun. However your proposition seems fair and I think that my people will accept it and will retire to the reservation you offer them. Then we will dwell apart in peace, for the words of the Great White Chief seem to be the words of nature speaking to my people out of dense darkness.

It matters little where we pass the remnant of our days. They will not be many. The Indian's night promises to be dark. Not a single star of hope hovers above his horizon. Sad-voiced winds moan in the distance. Grim fate seems to be on the Red Man's trail, and wherever he goes he will hear the approaching footsteps of his fell destroyer and prepare stolidly to meet his doom, as does the wounded doe that hears the approaching footsteps of the hunter.

A few more moons, a few more winters, and not one of the descendants of the mighty hosts that once moved over this broad land or lived in happy homes, protected by the Great Spirit, will remain to mourn over the graves of a people once more powerful and hopeful than yours. But why should I mourn at the untimely fate of my people? Tribe follows tribe, and nation follows nation, like the waves of the sea. It is the order of nature and regret is useless. Your time of decay may be distant, but it will surely come, for even the White Man whose God walked and talked with him as friend to friend, cannot be exempt from the common destiny. We may be brothers after all. We will see.

We will ponder your proposition and when we decide we will let you know. But should we accept it, I here and now make this condition that we will not be denied the privilege without molestation of visiting at any time the tombs of our ancestors, friends, and children. Every part of this soil is sacred in the estimation of my people. Every hillside, every valley, every plain and grove has been hallowed by some sad or happy event in days long vanished. Even the rocks, which seem to be dumb and dead as they swelter in the sun along the silent shore, thrill with memories of stirring events connected with the lives of my people, and the very dust upon which you now stand responds more lovingly to their footsteps than yours, because it is rich with the blood of our ancestors, and our bare feet are conscious of the sympathetic touch. Our departed braves, fond mothers, glad, happy hearted maidens, and even the little children who lived here and rejoiced here for a brief season, will love these sombre solitudes and at eventide they greet shadowy returning spirits. And when the last Red Man shall have perished and the memory of my tribe shall have become a myth among the White Men, these shores will swarm with the invisible dead of my tribe, and when your children's children think themselves alone in the field, the store, the shop, upon the highway, or in the silence of the pathless wood, they will not be alone.

Speech to the Commissioner of Indian Affairs, by Chief Seathl, 1854

9

DEEP PEACE OF THE RUNNING WAVE

Deep peace of the Running Wave to you.
Deep peace of the Flowing Air to you.
Deep peace of the Quiet Earth to you.
Deep peace of the Shining Stars to you.
Deep peace of the Son of Peace to you.

A Celtic Blessing, author and date unknown

10

THANKSGIVINGS FOR THE BODY

O Lord!
Thou hast given me a Body,
Wherein the glory of thy Power shineth,
Wonderfully composed above the Beasts,
Within distinguished into useful parts,
Beautified without with many Ornaments.
Limbs rarely poised,
And made for Heaven:

Arteries filled
With celestial Spirits;
Veins, wherein Blood floweth
Refreshing all my flesh,
Like Rivers.
Sinews fraught with the mystery
Of wonderful Strength,
Stability,
Feeling.
O blessed be thy glorious Name!
That thou hast made it,
A Treasury of Wonders,
Fit for its several Ages,
For Dissections,
For Sculptures in Brass,
For Draughts in Anatomy,
For the Contemplation of the Sages …

The spacious Room
Which thou hast hidden in mine Eye,
The Chambers for Sounds
Which thou hast prepar'd in mine Ear,
The Receptacles for Smells
Concealed in my Nose;
The feeling of my Hands
The taste of my Tongue.

But above all, O Lord, the Glory of Speech, whereby thy Servant is enabled with Praise to celebrate thee.

For
All the Beauties in Heaven and Earth,
The melody of Sounds,
The sweet Odours
Of thy Dwelling-place.
The delectable pleasures that gratifie my Sense
That gratify the feeling of Mankind.
The Light of History,
Admitted by the Ear.
The Light of Heaven,
Brought in by the Eye.
The Volubility and Liberty
Of my Hands and Members.
Fitted by thee for all Operations;
Which the Fancy can imagine,
Or Soul desire:
From the framing of a Needle's Eye,
To the building of a Tower:
From the squaring of Trees,
To the polishing of Kings' Crowns …

From 'A Serious and Pathetical Contemplation of the Mercies of God' by Thomas Traherne, 1699

11

THANKING GOD FOR THE BODY'S PASSAGES

Blessed are You – the Lord our God, King of the universe, who has formed man in wisdom, and created in him many orifices and hollow passages. It is revealed and known before Your glorious throne, that should any one of those be opened or any one of those be closed, it would be impossible for man to survive or stand before You. Blessed are You – the Lord, who heals all flesh and performs wonders.

From *The Jewish Authorised Daily Prayer Book*, current edition

12

ST BENNO AND THE FROG

It was often the habit of the man of God to go about the fields in meditation and prayer: and once as he passed by a certain marsh, a talkative frog was croaking in its slimey waters: and lest it should disturb his contemplation, he bade it to be a Seraphian, in as much as all the frogs in Seraphus are mute. But when he had gone on a little way, he called to mind the saying in Daniel: '*O ye whales and all that move in the waters, bless ye the Lord. O all ye beasts and cattle, bless ye the Lord.*' And fearing lest the singing of the frogs might be more agreeable to God than his own praying, he again issued his command to them, that they should praise God in their accustomed fashion: and soon the air and the fields were vehement with their conversation.

From *Beasts and Saints*, trans. Helen Waddell, 1934

13

ST GODRIC AND THE REPTILES

The gentleness of his heart did not betray itself only in kindness to men, but his wise solicitude watched over the very reptiles and the creatures of the earth. For in winter when all was frozen stiff in the cold, he would go out barefoot, and if he lighted on any animal helpless with misery of the cold, he would set it under his armpit or in his bosom to warm it. Many a time would the kind soul go spying under the thick hedges or tangled patches of briars, and if haply he found a creature that had lost its way, or cowed with the harshness of the weather, or tired, or half dead, he would recover it with all the healing art he had ...

And if anyone in his service had caught a bird or a little beast in a snare or a trap or a noose, as soon as he found it he would snatch it from their hands and let it go free in the fields or the glades of the wood …

From *Beasts and Saints*, trans. Helen Waddell, 1934

14

ST KEVIN AND THE BLACKBIRD

At one Lenten season, St Kevin, as was his way, fled from the company of men to a certain solitude, and in a little hut that did but keep out the sun and the rain, gave himself earnestly to reading and to prayer, and his leisure to contemplation alone. And as he knelt in his accustomed fashion, with his hand outstretched through the window and lifted up to heaven, a blackbird settled on it, and busying herself as in her nest, laid in it an egg. And so moved was the saint that in all patience and gentleness he remained, neither closing nor withdrawing his hand: but until the young ones were fully hatched he held it out unwearied, shaping it for the purpose. And for a sign of perpetual remembrance of this thing, all the images of St Kevin throughout Ireland, show a blackbird in his outstretched hand.

From *Beasts and Saints*, trans. Helen Waddell, 1934

15

THE PROPHET MUHAMMAD AND THE BABY BIRDS

A man came before the Prophet with a carpet, and said, 'O Prophet! I passed through a wood, and heard the voices of young birds; and I took them and put them into my carpet; and their mother came fluttering round my head, and I uncovered the young, and the mother fell down upon them, then I wrapped them up in my carpet; and here are the young which I have.' Then the Prophet said, 'Put them down.' And when he did so, their mother joined them: and the Prophet Muhammad said, 'Do you wonder at the affection of the mother towards her young? I swear by Him who hath sent me, verily God is more loving to his creatures than the mother to these young birds. Return them to the place from which you took them, and let their mother be with them.'

One of the *Hadith*, the collection of the Prophet Muhammad's sayings

16

THE WONDER OF THE BEHEMOTH

Behold now behemoth, which I made with thee; he eateth grass as an ox.

Lo now, his strength is in his loins, and his force is in the navel of his belly.

He moveth his tail like a cedar: the sinews of his stones are wrapped together.

His bones are as strong pieces of brass; his bones are like bars of iron.

He is the chief of the ways of God: he that made him can make his sword to approach unto him.

Surely the mountains bring him forth food, where all the beasts of the field play.

He lieth under the shady trees, in the covert of the reed, and fens.

The shady trees cover him with their shadow; the willows of the brook compass him about.

Behold, he drinketh up a river, and hasteth not: he trusteth that he can draw up Jordan into his mouth.

He taketh it with his eyes: his nose pierceth through snares.

Job 40:15–24

17

A PRAYER FOR ANIMALS

O God enlarge within us a sense of fellowship with all living things, our brothers and sisters, to whom you gave the earth as their home in common with us. May we realise that they live not for us alone but for themselves and for you, and that they love the sweetness of life.

Prayer of St Basil, fourth century

CHAPTER TWO

THE WAY OF THE MYSTIC

THE PASSAGES THAT FOLLOW ARE *some of the most glorious and most difficult in this book. The writers are struggling to express in human language what cannot be expressed in words. I am not a mystic and some of these passages I find very disquieting, even shocking. Yet it seems to me that they struggle to say something very important. I would not claim to understand any of these passages fully, but in some way I glimpse a meaning in them which matters to me.*

18

THE VALLEY OF THE DRY BONES

The hand of the LORD was upon me, and carried me out in the spirit of the LORD, and set me down in the midst of the valley which was full of bones,

And caused me to pass by them round about: and, behold, there were very many in the open valley; and, lo, they were very dry.

And he said unto me, Son of man, can these bones live? And I answered, O Lord GOD, thou knowest.

Again he said unto me, Prophesy upon these bones, and say unto them, O ye dry bones, hear the word of the LORD.

Thus saith the Lord GOD unto these bones; Behold, I will cause breath to enter into you, and ye shall live:

And I will lay sinews upon you, and will bring up flesh upon you, and cover you with skin, and put breath in you, and ye shall live; and ye shall know that I am the LORD.

So I prophesied as I was commanded: and as I prophesied, there was a noise, and behold a shaking, and the bones came together, bone to his bone.

And when I beheld, lo, the sinews and the flesh came up upon them, and the skin covered them above: but there was no breath in them.

Then said he unto me, Prophesy unto the wind, prophesy, son

of man, and say to the wind, Thus saith the Lord GOD; Come from the four winds, O breath, and breathe upon these slain, that they may live.

So I prophesied as he commanded me, and the breath came into them, and they lived, and stood up upon their feet, an exceeding great army.

Then he said unto me, Son of man, these bones are the whole house of Israel: behold, they say, Our bones are dried, and our hope is lost: we are cut off for our parts.

Therefore prophesy and say unto them, Thus saith the Lord GOD; Behold, O my people, I will open your graves, and cause you to come up out of your graves, and bring you into the land of Israel.

And ye shall know that I am the LORD, when I have opened your graves, O my people, and brought you up out of your graves,

And shall put my spirit in you, and ye shall live, and I shall place you in your own land: then shall ye know that I the LORD have spoken it, and performed it, saith the LORD.

Ezekiel 37:1–14

19

TRYING TO UNDERSTAND GOD

God what shall I say thou art when thou canst not be named? What shall I speak of thee, when in speaking of thee, I speak nothing but contradiction? ...

Nay, I see that God is in all creatures, man and beast, fish and fowl, and every green thing, from the highest cedar to the ivy on the wall; and that God is the life and being of them all, and that God doth really dwell, and if you will personally; if he may admit so low an expression in them all, and hath his being no where else out of the creatures.

Further, I see that all the beings in the world are but that our being, and so he may well be said, to be every where as he is, and so I cannot exclude him from man or beast, or any other creature: every creature and thing having that being living in it, and there is no difference betwixt man and beast; but as man carries a more lively image of the divine being than any other creature: for I see the power, wisdom and glory of God in one, as well as another, only in that creature called man, God appears more gloriously than the rest.

And truly, I find by experience, the grand reason why I have, and many others do now use set times of prayer, and run to formal duties, and other outward and low service of God: the reason hath been, and is, because men look upon a God as being without them and remote from them at a great distance, as if he were locally in heaven, and sitting there only, and would not let down any blessing or good things, but by such and such a way and means.

But Lord, how carnal was I thus to fancy thee? Nay, I am confident, that there is never a man under the sun that looks upon God in such a form: but must be a gross idolator, and fancy some corporal shape of him, though they may call it spiritual …

I shall speak my own experience herein, that I have made God mutable as my self, and therefore as things and conditions have changed, I thought that God was angry or pleased, and to have fallen a humbling my self; or otherwise in thankfulness, never looking or considering that God is one entire perfect and immutable being, and that all things were according to the counsel of his own will, and did serve the design of his own glory; but thought that my sins or holy walking did cause him to alter his purpose of good or evil to me.

But now I cannot look upon any condition or action, but methinks there appears a sweet concurrence of the supreme will in it; nothing comes short of it, or goes beyond it, nor any man shall do or be any thing, but what shall fall in a sweet compliance with it; it being the womb wherein all things are conceived, and in which all creatures were formed and brought forth.

Yea, further, there is not the least flower or herb in the field but there is the divine being in it by which it is, that which it is; and as that departs out of it, so it comes to nothing, and so it is today clothed by God, and tomorrow cast into the oven: when God ceases to live in it then it comes to nothing, and so all the visible creatures are lively resemblances of the divine being. But if this be so, some may say: 'Then look how many creatures there are in the world, there is so many Gods, and when they die and perish, then must God also die with them, which can be no less than blasphemy to affirm.'

To which I answer, and it is apparent to me, that all the creatures in the world; they are not so many distinct beings, but they are but one entire being, though they may be distinguished in respect of their forms; yet their being is but one and the same being, made out in so many forms of flesh, as men and beast, fish and fowl, trees and herbs: for though these two last trees and herbs have not the life so sensibly or lively; yet it is certain there is a life and being in them, by which they grow to that maturity and perfection, that they become serviceable for the use of man, as other creatures are; and yet I must not exclude God from them; for as God is pleased to dwell in flesh, and to dwell with and in man, yet is he not flesh, nor doth the flesh partake of the divine Being. Only this, God is pleased to live in flesh, and as the scripture saith, he is made flesh; and he appears in several forms of flesh, in the form of man and beast, and other creatures, and when these have performed the design and will of God, that then as the flesh of man and other creatures, came from the earth, and are not capable of knowing God, or partaking of the divine nature, and God ceasing to live in them, and being gone out of them, that then they shall return to their first principle of dust, and God shall as he did from all eternity, live in himself, before there was a world or creatures; so he shall to all eternity live and enjoy himself in himself, in such a way as no man can utter: and so I see him yesterday, and today, and the same for ever: the alpha and the omega, the beginning and the end of all things …

From *The Light and Dark Sides of God* by Jacob Bauthumley, c. 1650

20

IN THE BEGINNING WAS THE WORD

In the beginning was the Word, and the Word was with God, and the Word was God.
The same was in the beginning with God.
All things were made by him; and without him was not any thing made that was made.
In him was life; and the life was the light of men.
And the light shineth in darkness; and the darkness comprehended it not.
There was a man sent from God, whose name was John.
The same came for a witness, to bear witness of the Light, that all men through him might believe.
He was not that Light, but was sent to bear witness of that Light.

That was the true Light, which lighteth every man that cometh into the world.

He was in the world, and the world was made by him, and the world knew him not.

He came unto his own, and his own received him not.

But as many as received him, to them gave he power to become the sons of God, even to them that believe on his name:

Which were born, not of blood, nor of the will of the flesh, nor of the will of man, but of God.

And the Word was made flesh, and dwelt among us, (and we beheld his glory, the glory as of the only begotten of the Father,) full of grace and truth.

The Gospel of St John 1:1–14

21

TAO – THE WAY AND ITS POWER

The Way that can be told of is not an Unvarying Way;
The names that can be named are not unvarying names.
It was from the Nameless that Heaven and Earth sprang;
The named is but the mother that rears the ten thousand creatures, each after its kind.

Truly, 'Only he that rids himself forever of desire can see the Secret Essences';
He that has never rid himself of desire can see only the Outcomes.
These two things issued from the same mould, but nevertheless are different in name.
This 'same mould' we can but call the Mystery,
Or rather the 'darker than any Mystery',
The Doorway whence issued all Secret Essences …

The Way is like an empty vessel
That yet may be drawn from
Without ever needing to be filled.
It is bottomless; the very progenitor of all things in the world.
In it all sharpness is blunted,
All tangles untied,
All glare tempered,
All dust smoothed.
It is like a deep pool that never dries.
Was it too the child of something else? We cannot tell …

We put thirty spokes together and call it a wheel;
But it is on the space where there is nothing that the utility of the wheel depends.
We turn clay to make a vessel;
But it is on the space where there is nothing that the utility of the vessel depends.
We pierce doors and windows to make a house;

And it is on these spaces where there is nothing that the utility of the house depends.

Therefore just as we take advantage of what is, we should recognise the utility of what is not.

From the *Tao Te Ching* by Lao Tzu, fifth century BC

22

JULIAN OF NORWICH IS SHOWN A LITTLE THING

At the same time, our Lord showed me, a spiritual sight of His homely loving.

I saw that He is to us everything that is good and comfortable for us: He is our clothing that for love wraps us, clasps us, and all encloses us for tender love, that He may never leave us; being to us all-thing that is good, as to mine understanding.

Also in this He showed me a little thing, the quantity of a hazel-nut in the palm of my hand; and it was as round as a ball. I looked thereupon with eye of my understanding, and thought: *What may this be?* And it was answered generally thus: *It is all that is made*. I marvelled how it might last, for I thought it might suddenly have fallen to naught for littleness. And I was answered in my understanding; *It lasts, and ever shall last for that God loves it*. And so all-thing hath the being by the love of God.

In this little thing I saw three properties. The first is that God made it, the second is that God loves it, the third, that God keeps it. But what is to me verily the Maker, the Keeper, and the Lover, – I cannot tell; for till I am substantially oned to [i.e. united with] Him, I may never have full rest nor very bliss: that is to say, till I be so fastened to Him, that there is right nought that is made betwixt my God and me.

It needs us to have knowing of the littleness of creatures and to hold as nought all-thing that is made, for to love and have God that is unmade. For this is the cause why we be not all in ease of heart and soul: that we seek here rest in those things that are so little, wherein is no rest, and know not our God that is All-mighty, All-wise, All-good …

From *Revelations of Divine Love* by Julian of Norwich, fourteenth century

23

SOME PROVERBS OF PARADOX

A fool sees not the same tree that a wise man sees.
He whose face gives no light, shall never become a star.
Eternity is in love with the productions of time.
All wholesome food is caught without a net or a trap.
No bird soars too high, if he soars with his own wings.
The most sublime act is to set another before you.
If the fool would persist in his folly he would become wise.
Folly is the cloak of knavery.
Shame is pride's cloak.
Prisons are built with stones of law, brothels with bricks of religion.
The pride of the peacock is the glory of God.
The lust of the goat is the bounty of God.
The wrath of the lion is the wisdom of God.
The nakedness of woman is the work of God.
Excess of sorrow laughs. Excess of joy weeps.
The roaring of lions, the howling of wolves, the raging of the stormy sea, and the destructive sword, are portions of eternity too great for the eye of man.
The fox condemns the trap, not himself.
Joys impregnate. Sorrows bring forth.

The bird a nest, the spider a web, man friendship.

One thought fills immensity.

Always be ready to speak your mind, and a base man will avoid you.

Everything possible to be believed is an image of truth.

The eagle never lost so much time, as when he submitted to learn of the crow.

As the plough follows words, so God rewards prayers.

The tigers of wrath are wiser than the horse of instruction.

Expect poison from standing water.

You never know what is enough unless you know what is more than enough.

Listen to the fool's reproach! It is a kingly title!

The eyes of fire, the nostrils of air, the mouth of water, the beard of earth.

The apple tree never asks the beech how he shall grow; nor the lion, the horse, how he shall take his prey.

The thankful receiver bears a plentiful harvest.

If others had not been foolish, we should be so.

The soul of sweet delight can never be defiled.

When thou seest an eagle, thou seest a portion of genius. Lift up thy head!

To create a little flower is the labour of ages.

Damn braces; bless relaxes.

The best wine is the oldest, the best water the newest.

The head sublime the heart pathos, the genitals beauty, the hands and feet proportion.

The crow wished everything was black, the owl that everything was white.
Exuberance is beauty.

From *The Marriage of Heaven and Hell* by William Blake, 1790

24

LEARNING FROM A LITTLE CHILD

At the same time came the disciples unto Jesus, saying, Who is the greatest in the kingdom of heaven?
And Jesus called a little child unto him, and set him in the midst of them,
And said, Verily I say unto you, Except ye be converted, and become as little children, ye shall not enter into the kingdom of heaven.
Whosoever therefore shall humble himself as this little child, the same is greatest in the kingdom of heaven.
And whoso shall receive one such little child in my name receiveth me.
But whoso shall offend one of these little ones which believe in me, it were better for him that a millstone were hanged about his neck, and that he were drowned in the depth of the sea.

The Gospel of St Matthew 18:1–6

25

PAGAN NATURE MYSTICISM

The High Priest:
Hear ye the words of the Star Goddess; she in the dust of whose feet are the hosts of heaven, whose body encircles the universe.
The High Priestess:
I who am the beauty of the green earth, and the white moon among the stars, and the mystery of the waters, and the desire of the heart of man, call unto thy soul.

Arise, and come unto me. For I am the soul of nature, who gives life to the universe. From me, all things proceed and unto me all things must return; and before my face, beloved of Gods and of men, let thine innermost divine self be enfolded in the rapture of the infinite.

Let my worship be within the heart that rejoiceth; for behold, all acts of love and pleasure are my rituals. And therefore let there be beauty and strength; power and compassion, honour and humility, mirth and reverence within you.

And thou who thinkest to seek for me, know thy seeking and yearning shall avail thee not unless thou knowest the mystery: that if that which thou seekest thou findest not within thee, thou wilt never find it without thee. For behold,

I have been with thee from the beginning; and I am that which is attained at the end of desire.

From *The Pagan Charge* of Wicca, twentieth century

26

EARTH MYSTERY AND MYSTICISM

The story of my heart commences seventeen years ago. In the glow of youth there were times every now and then when I felt the necessity of a strong inspiration of soul-thought. My heart was dusty, parched for want of the rain of deep feeling; my mind arid and dry, for there is a dust which settles on the heart as well as that which falls on a ledge. It is injurious to the mind as well as to the body to be always in one place and always surrounded by the same circumstances. A species of thick clothing slowly grows about the mind, the pores are choked, little habits become a part of existence, and by degrees the mind is inclosed in a husk. When this began to form I felt eager to escape from it, to throw it off like heavy clothing, to drink deeply once more at the fresh fountains of life. An inspiration – a long deep breath of the pure air of thought – could alone give health to the heart.

There was a hill to which I used to resort at such periods. The labour of walking three miles to it, all the while gradually ascending, seemed to clear my blood of the heaviness accumulated at home. On a warm summer day the slow continued rise required continual effort, which carried away the sense of oppression. The familiar everyday scene was soon out of sight; I came to other trees, meadows, and fields; I began to breathe a new air and to have a fresher aspiration. I restrained my soul till I reached the sward of the hill; psyche, the soul that longed to be loose. I would write psyche always instead of soul to avoid meanings which have become attached to the word soul, but it is awkward to do so. Clumsy indeed are all words the moment the wooden stage of commonplace life is left. I restrained psyche, my soul, till I reached and put my foot on the grass at the beginning of the green hill itself.

Moving up the sweet short turf, at every step my heart seemed to obtain a wider horizon of feeling; with every inhalation of rich pure air, a deeper desire. The very light of the sun was whiter and more brilliant here. By the time I had reached the summit I had entirely forgotten the petty circumstances and the annoyances of existence. I felt myself, myself. There was an intrenchment on the summit, and going down into the fosse I walked round it slowly to recover breath. On the south-western side there was a spot where the outer bank had partially slipped, leaving a gap. There the view was over a broad plain, beautiful with wheat and inclosed by a perfect amphitheatre of green hills. Through these hills there was one narrow groove, or pass, southwards, where the white clouds seem to close into the horizon. Woods hid the scattered hamlets and farmhouses, so that I was quite alone.

I was utterly alone with the sun and the earth. Lying down on the grass, I spoke in my soul to the earth, the sun, the air, and the distant sea far beyond sight. I thought of the earth's firmness – I felt it bear me up; through the grassy couch there came an influence as if I could feel the great earth speaking to me. I thought of the wandering air – its pureness, which is its beauty; the air touched me and gave me something of itself. I spoke to the sea: though so far, in my mind I saw it, green at the rim of the earth and blue in deeper ocean; I desired to have its strength, its mystery and glory. Then I addressed the sun, desiring the soul equivalent of his light and brilliance, his endurance and unwearied race. I turned to the blue heaven over, gazing into its depth, inhaling its exquisite colour and sweetness. The rich blue of the unattainable flower of the sky drew my soul towards it, and there it rested, for pure colour is rest of heart. By all these I prayed: I felt an emotion of the soul beyond all definition; prayer is a puny thing to it, and the word is a rude sign to the feeling, but I know no other.

By the blue heaven, by the rolling sun bursting through untrodden space, a new ocean of ether every day unveiled. By the fresh and wandering air encompassing the world; by the sea sounding on the shore – the green sea white-flecked at the margin and the deep ocean; by the strong earth under me. Then, returning, I prayed by the sweet thyme, whose little flowers I touched with my hand; by the slender grass; by the crumble of dry chalky earth I took up and let fall through my fingers. Touching the crumble of earth, the blade of grass, the thyme flower, breathing the earth-encircling air, thinking of the sea and the sky, holding out my hand for the sunbeams to touch it, prone on the sward in token of deep reverence, thus I prayed that I might touch to the unutterable existence infinitely higher than deity.

From *The Story of My Heart* by Richard Jefferies, 1883

CHAPTER THREE

HOW TO LIVE AND WORK

HERE ARE THE PASSAGES WHICH LAY down the essentials of the spiritual in daily life. Some of them, like the Ten Commandments, are pocket guides to religious and social life. Others emphasise essential priorities for those who wish to live a life which is not merely one of acquisition and pleasure-seeking. All of these passages address those, like myself, leading ordinary lives, coping with the ordinary stresses of the world.

27

LOOK TO THIS DAY

Look to this day! For it is life, the very life of life. In its brief course lie all the varieties and realities of your existence: the bliss of growth, the glory of action, the splendour of beauty. For yesterday is already a dream and tomorrow is only a vision, but today, well lived, makes every yesterday a dream of happiness and every tomorrow a vision of hope. Look well, therefore, to this day! Such is the salutation of the dawn.

From the Sanskrit, author and date unknown

28

THE TEN COMMANDMENTS

And God spake all these words, saying,

I am the LORD thy God, which have brought thee out of the land of Egypt, out of the house of bondage.

1. Thou shalt have no other gods before me.

2. Thou shalt not make unto thee any graven image, or any likeness of any thing that is in heaven above, or that is in the earth beneath, or that is in the water under the earth: Thou shalt not bow down thyself to them, nor serve them: for I the LORD thy God am a jealous God, visiting the iniquity of the fathers upon the children unto the third and fourth generation of them that hate me; and shewing mercy unto thousands of them that love me, and keep my commandments.

3. Thou shalt not take the name of the LORD thy God in vain; for the LORD will not hold him guiltless that taketh his name in vain.

4. Remember the sabbath day, to keep it holy. Six days shalt thou labour, and do all thy work: but the seventh day is the sabbath of the LORD thy God: in it thou shalt not do any work, thou, nor thy son, nor thy daughter, thy manservant, nor thy maidservant, nor thy cattle, nor thy stranger that is within thy gates: for in six days the LORD made heaven and earth, the sea, and all that in them is, and rested the seventh day: wherefore the LORD blessed the sabbath day, and hallowed it.

5. Honour thy father and thy mother: that thy days may be long upon the land which the LORD thy God giveth thee.

6. Thou shalt not kill.

7. Thou shalt not commit adultery.

8. Thou shalt not steal.

9. Thou shalt not bear false witness against thy neighbour.

10. Thou shalt not covet thy neighbour's house, thou shalt not covet thy neighbour's wife, nor his manservant, nor his maidservant, nor his ox, nor his ass, nor any thing that is thy neighbour's.

Exodus 20:1–17

29

JESUS GIVES THE SERMON ON THE MOUNT

And seeing the multitudes, he went up into a mountain: and when he was set, his disciples came unto him:
And he opened his mouth, and taught them, saying,
Blessed are the poor in spirit: for theirs is the kingdom of heaven.
Blessed are they that mourn: for they shall be comforted.
Blessed are the meek: for they shall inherit the earth.
Blessed are they which do hunger and thirst after righteousness: for they shall be filled.

Blessed are the merciful: for they shall obtain mercy.

Blessed are the pure in heart: for they shall see God.

Blessed are the peacemakers: for they shall be called the children of God.

Blessed are they which are persecuted for righteousness' sake: for theirs is the kingdom of heaven.

Blessed are ye, when men shall revile you, and persecute you, and shall say all manner of evil against you falsely, for my sake.

Rejoice, and be exceeding glad: for great is your reward in heaven: for so persecuted they the prophets which were before you.

Ye are the salt of the earth: but if the salt have lost his savour, wherewith shall it be salted? it is thenceforth good for nothing, but to be cast out, and to be trodden under foot of men.

Ye are the light of the world. A city that is set on an hill cannot be hid.

Neither do men light a candle, and put it under a bushel, but on a candlestick; and it giveth light unto all that are in the house.

Let your light so shine before men, that they may see your good works, and glorify your Father which is in heaven.

Think not that I am come to destroy the law, or the prophets: I am not come to destroy, but to fulfil.

For verily I say unto you, Till heaven and earth pass, one jot or one tittle shall in no wise pass from the law, till all be fulfilled.

Whosoever therefore shall break one of these least commandments, and shall teach men so, he shall be called the least in the kingdom of heaven: but whosoever shall do and teach them, the same shall be called great in the kingdom of heaven.

For I say unto you, That except your righteousness shall exceed the righteousness of the scribes and Pharisees, ye shall in no case enter into the kingdom of heaven.

Ye have heard that it was said by them of old time, Thou shalt not kill; and whosoever shall kill shall be in danger of the judgment:

But I say unto you, That whosoever is angry with his brother without a cause shall be in danger of the judgment: and whosoever shall say to his brother, Raca, shall be in danger of the council: but whosoever shall say, Thou fool, shall be in danger of hell fire.

Therefore if thou bring thy gift to the altar, and there rememberest that thy brother hath ought against thee;

Leave there thy gift before the altar, and go thy way; first be reconciled to thy brother, and then come and offer thy gift.

Agree with thine adversary quickly, whiles thou art in the way with him; lest at any time the adversary deliver thee to the judge, and the judge deliver thee to the officer, and thou be cast into prison.

Verily I say unto thee, Thou shalt by no means come out thence, till thou hast paid the uttermost farthing.

Ye have heard that it was said by them of old time, Thou shalt not commit adultery:

But I say unto you, That whosoever looketh on a woman to lust after her hath committed adultery with her already in his heart.

And if thy right eye offend thee, pluck it out, and cast it from thee: for it is profitable for thee that one of thy members should perish, and not that thy whole body should be cast into hell.

And if thy right hand offend thee, cut it off, and cast it from thee: for it is profitable for thee that one of thy members should perish, and not that thy whole body should be cast into hell.

It hath been said, Whosoever shall put away his wife, let him give her a writing of divorcement:

But I say unto you, That whosoever shall put away his wife, saving for the cause of fornication, causeth her to commit adultery: and whosoever shall marry her that is divorced committeth adultery.

Again, ye have heard that it hath been said by them of old time, Thou shalt not forswear thyself, but shalt perform unto the Lord thine oaths:

But I say unto you, Swear not at all; neither by heaven; for it is God's throne:

Nor by the earth; for it is his footstool: neither by Jerusalem; for it is the city of the great King.

Neither shalt thou swear by thy head, because thou canst not make one hair white or black.

But let your communication be, Yea, yea; Nay, nay: for whatsoever is more than these cometh of evil.

Ye have heard that it hath been said, An eye for an eye, and a tooth for a tooth:

But I say unto you, That ye resist not evil: but whosoever shall smite thee on thy right cheek, turn to him the other also.

And if any man will sue thee at the law, and take away thy coat, let him have thy cloak also.

And whosoever shall compel thee to go a mile, go with him twain.

Give to him that asketh thee, and from him that would borrow of thee turn not thou away.

Ye have heard that it hath been said, Thou shalt love thy neighbour, and hate thine enemy.

But I say unto you, Love your enemies, bless them that curse you, do good to them that hate you, and pray for them which despitefully use you, and persecute you;

That ye may be the children of your Father which is in heaven: for he maketh his sun to rise on the evil and on the good, and sendeth rain on the just and on the unjust.

For if ye love them which love you, what reward have ye? do not even the publicans the same?

And if ye salute your brethren only, what do ye more than others? do not even the publicans so?

Be ye therefore perfect, even as your Father which is in heaven is perfect.

The Gospel of St Matthew 5:1–48

30

ARJUNA THE WARRIOR ASKS THE GOD KRISHNA HOW TO LIVE

Arjuna, the warrior, is fighting a battle. He realises that he does not wish to kill his foes, who include his relatives and even his teachers. For a moment he refuses to fight. The Lord Krishna is acting as his charioteer and Arjuna turns to him, asks him to be his guru, then starts asking about wisdom.

Arjuna speaks:
Tell me of those who live established in wisdom, ever aware of the Self, O Krishna. How do they talk? How sit? How move about?

Sri Krishna:
They live in wisdom who see themselves in all and all in them, who have renounced every selfish desire and sense craving tormenting the heart.

Neither agitated by grief nor hankering after pleasure, they live free from lust and fear and anger. Established in meditation, they are truly wise. Fettered no more by selfish attachments, they are neither elated by good fortune nor depressed by bad. Such are the seers.

Even as a tortoise draws in its limbs, the wise can draw in their sense at will. Aspirants abstain from sense pleasures, but they still crave for them. These cravings all disappear when they see the highest goal. Even of those who tread the path, the stormy senses can sweep off the mind. They live in wisdom who subdue their senses and keep their minds ever absorbed in me.

When you keep thinking about sense objects, attachment comes. Attachment breeds desire, the lust of possession that burns to anger. Anger clouds the judgement; you can no longer learn from past mistakes. Lost is the power to choose between what is wise and what is unwise, and your life is utter waste. But when you move amidst the world of sense, free from attachment and aversion alike, there comes the peace in which all sorrows end, and you live in the wisdom of the Self.

The disunited mind is far from wise; how can it meditate? How be at peace? When you know no peace, how can you know joy? When you let your mind follow the call of the senses, they carry away your better judgment as storms drive a boat off its charted course on the sea.

Use all your power to free the senses from attachment and aversion alike, and live in the full wisdom of the Self. Such a sage awakes to light in the night of all creatures. That which the world calls day is the night of ignorance to the wise.

As rivers flow into the ocean but cannot make the vast ocean overflow, so flow the streams of the sense-world into the sea of peace that is the sage. But this is not so with the desirer of desires.

They are forever free who renounce all selfish desires and break away from the ego-cage of 'I', 'me', and 'mine' to be united with the Lord. This is the supreme state. Attain to this, and pass from death to immortality.

The 'Bhagavad-Gita', 2, 54–71

31

STARTING EACH DAY THE STOIC WAY

Begin the morning by saying to yourself, 'Today I shall meet meddling, ungrateful, arrogant, deceitful, envious, antisocial men. All these things happen to them because of their ignorance of what is good and evil. But I who have seen the nature of the good, that it is beautiful, and of the bad, that it is ugly, and that the nature of him who does wrong is akin to me, (not just of the same blood or seed, but also in the same intelligence and the same portion of the divinity); I can neither be injured by any of them, for nobody can involve me in wrong, nor can I be angry with my kinsman, or hate him. For we are made for co-operations, like feet, like hands, like eyelids, like the rows of the upper and lower teeth. To act against each other then is contrary to nature; and it is acting against each other to let oneself be vexed and to turn away …

Every moment think steadily as a Roman and a man, to do

what you have in hand with perfect and simple dignity, and feeling of affection, and freedom and justice; and to give yourself repose from all other thoughts. And you will give yourself this repose, if you do every act of your life as if it were the last, laying aside all carelessness and passionate aversion from the commands of reason, and all hypocrisy, and self-love, and discontent with the portion which has been given to you. You see how few things a man needs to practise in order to live a life which flows in quiet, and is like the existence of the gods; for the gods on their part will require nothing more from him who observes these things …

Do the external things distract you? Give yourself time to learn something new and good, and cease to be whirled around. But after this, you must also avoid being carried off in the other direction. For those too are triflers who have wearied themselves in life by their activity, and yet have no object to which to direct every movement, and, in a word, all their thoughts.

A man has seldom been unhappy through not observing what is in the mind of another; but those who do not observe the movements of their own minds, must of necessity be unhappy …

Men seek retreats for themselves, houses in the country, seashores, and mountains; and you too have a tendency to desire such things very much. But this is altogether a mark of the most common sort of men, for it is in your power whenever you will choose to retire into yourself. For nowhere does a man retire with more quiet or more freedom from trouble than into his own soul, particularly when he has within him such thoughts that by looking into them he is immediately in perfect tranquillity; and I affirm that tranquillity is nothing else than the good ordering of the mind. Then constantly give to yourself this retreat, and renew yourself; and let your principles be brief and fundamental, which, as soon as you go back to them, will be sufficient to cleanse the soul completely, and to send you back free from all discontent with the things to which you return.

For what is it that makes you discontented? The wickedness of men? Recall to your mind the precept, that rational creatures exist for one another, and that patience is part of justice, that men do wrong involuntarily; and how many already, by mutual enmity, suspicion, hatred and fighting, have been stretched out dead, reduced to ashes. Then be quiet again …

This then remains; remember to retire into this little territory of your own, and above all do not distract or strain yourself, but be free, and look at things like a man, like a human being, like a citizen, like a mortal. But among the things readiest to your hand to which you will turn, let there be these two. One is that things do not touch the soul, for they are external and cannot be altered; but our perturbations come only from our own thinking which is within us. The other is that all these things which you see, change immediately and will no longer exist; and constantly bear in mind how many of these changes you have already witnessed. The universe is change; life is opinion.

From *The Meditations* by Marcus Aurelius, second century AD

32

HOW THINKING LEADS TO HAPPINESS OR UNHAPPINESS

All that we are is the result of what we have thought: it is founded on our thoughts, it is made up of our thoughts. If a man speaks or acts with an evil thought, pain follows him, as the wheel follows the foot of the ox that draws the carriage.

All that we are is the result of what we have thought: it is founded on our thoughts, it is made up of our thoughts. If a man speaks or acts with a pure thought, happiness follows him, like a shadow that never leaves him.

'He abused me, he beat me, he defeated me, he robbed me,' – in those who harbour such thoughts hatred will never cease.

'He abused me, he beat me, he defeated me, he robbed me' – in those who do not harbour such thoughts hatred will cease.

For hatred does not cease by hatred at any time: hatred ceases by love – this is an old rule.

The world does not know that we must all come to an end here; but those who know it, their quarrels cease at once.

He who lives looking for pleasures only, his senses uncontrolled, immoderate in his food, idle and weak, Mara (the Tempter of evil spirit) will certainly overthrow him, as the wind throws down a weak tree.

He who lives without looking for pleasures, his senses well

controlled, moderate in his food, faithful and strong, Mara will certainly not overthrow him, any more than the wind throws down a rocky mountain …

As rain breaks through an ill-thatched house, passion will break through an unreflecting mind.

As rain does not break through a well-thatched house, passion will not break through a well-reflecting mind…

From *The Dhammapada*, fifth to first century BC

33

THE TAO AND THE ACTIONLESS WAY

Push far enough towards the Void,
Hold fast enough to Quietness,
And of the ten thousands things none but can be worked on
  by you.
I have beheld them, whither they go back.
See, all things howsoever they flourish
Return to the root from which they grew.
This return to the root is called Quietness;
Quietness is called submission to Fate;
What has submitted to Fate has become part of the always-so.
To know the always-so is to be Illumined;
Not to know it, means to go blindly to disaster.

He who knows the always-so has room in him for everything;
He who has room in him for everything is without prejudice.
To be without prejudice is to be kingly;
To be kingly is to be of heaven;
To be of heaven is to be in the Tao.
Tao is forever and he that possesses it,
Though his body ceases, is not destroyed ...

Fame or one's own self, which matters to one most?
One's own self or things bought, which should count most?
In the getting or the losing, which is worse?
Hence he who grudges expense pays dearest in the end;
He who has hoarded most will suffer the heaviest loss.
Be content with what you have and are, and no one can
despoil you;
Who stops in time nothing can harm.
He is forever safe and secure ...

Without leaving his door
He knows everything under heaven.
Without looking out of his window
He knows all the ways of heaven.
For the further one travels
The less one knows.
Therefore the Sage arrives without going,
Sees all without looking,
Does nothing, yet achieves everything.

From the *Tao Te Ching* by Lao Tzu, fifth century BC

34
THE JEWISH FATHERS' THOUGHTS ON LIVING

Hillel ... used to say: If I am not for myself, who will be for me? If I am only for myself, what am I? If not now, when? ... Hillel said: Do not separate yourself from the community. Trust not in yourself until the day of your death. Do not judge your fellow man until you have come into his situation. Do not say anything which cannot be understood at once, in the hope that it will be understood eventually. Do not say, When I have leisure I will study, for you may never have leisure.

Rabbi Elazar ben Azariah ... used to say: One whose wisdom exceeds his deeds, to what may he be compared? To a tree whose branches are many but whose roots are few, so that when the wind comes, it uproots it and overturns it; as it is said, He shall be like a lonely tree in the desert; when good comes he shall not see it; he shall dwell in the parched places of the desert, in a salt land that is not inhabited (Jeremiah 17:6). However, one whose deeds exceed his wisdom, to what may he be compared? To a tree whose branches are few but whose roots are many, so that even if all the world come and blow against it, they cannot move it from its place; as it is said, He shall be like a tree planted by waters, that sends out its roots by a stream and does not notice when the heat comes; its leaves are ever green; in a year of drought it is not troubled, and ceases not to bear fruit (Jeremiah 17:8)

Ben Zoma said: Who is wise? He who learns from every man; as it is said, From all my teachers I grew wise (Psalms 119:99). Who is mighty? He who masters his evil impulse; as it is said, He who is slow to anger is better than mighty, and he who rules over his spirit than he who conquers a city (Proverbs 16:22). Who is rich? He who is happy with his lot: as it is said, When you eat the labours of your hands, happy will you be and all will be well with you (Psalms 125:2). 'Happy will you be' – in this world – 'and all will be well with you' – in the world to come. Who is honoured? He who honours his fellow men; as it is said, I will honour those who honour Me; but those who despise Me shall be held in contempt (1 Samuel 2:30)

From 'Ethics of the Fathers' in *The Jewish Authorised Daily Prayer Book*, current edition

35

BEWARE SUPERFLUOUS WANTS AND DESIRES

The soul, when accustomed to superfluous things, acquires a strong habit of desiring others which are necessary neither for the preservation of the individual nor for that of the species. This desire is without limit; whilst things which are necessary are few, and restricted within certain bounds. Lay this well to heart, reflect on it again and again; that which is superfluous is without end (and therefore the desire for it also without limit). Thus you desire to have your vessels of silver, but golden vessels are still better; others even have vessels studded with sapphires, emeralds, or rubies. Those, therefore, who are ignorant of this truth, that the desire for superfluous things is without limit, are constantly in trouble and pain. When they thus meet with the consequence of their course, they complain of the judgments of God; they go so far as to say that God's power is insufficient, because He has given to this universe the properties which they imagine cause these evils.

Moses Maimonides, twelfth century

36

TODAY, TAKE HEAVEN

I am your friend and my love for you goes deep. There is nothing I can give you which you have not got, but there is much, very much, that, while I cannot give it, you can take.

No heaven can come to us unless our hearts find rest in today. Take heaven!

No peace lies in the future which is not hidden in this present little instant. Take peace!

The gloom of the world is but a shadow. Behind it, yet within our reach is joy. There is radiance and glory in the darkness could we but see – and to see we have only to look. I beseech you to look!

Life is so generous a giver, but we, judging its gifts by the covering, cast them away as ugly, or heavy or hard. Remove the covering and you will find beneath it a living splendour, woven of love, by wisdom, with power.

Welcome it, grasp it, touch the angel's hand that brings it to you. Everything we call a trial, a sorrow, or a duty, believe me, that angel's hand is there, the gift is there, and the wonder of an overshadowing presence. Our joys, too, be not content with them as joys. They, too, conceal diviner gifts.

Life is so full of meaning and purpose, so full of beauty –

beneath its covering – that you will find earth but cloaks your heaven.

Courage, then, to claim it, that is all. But courage you have, and the knowledge that we are all pilgrims together, wending through unknown country, home.

And so, at this time, I greet you. Not quite as the world sends greetings, but with profound esteem and with the prayer that for you now and forever, the day breaks, and the shadows flee away.

From a letter by Fra Giovanni Giocondo

37

BE PATTERNS, BE EXAMPLES

And this is the word of the Lord God to you all, and a charge to you all in the presence of the living God: be patterns, be examples in all countries, places, islands, nations, wherever you come, that your carriage and life may preach among all sorts of people, and to them; then you will come to walk cheerfully over the world, answering that of God in every one.

From a letter by George Fox in prison, 1656

38

PRACTICAL ADVICE ON CHANGING YOUR LIFE FOR GOOD

Reader, whether young or old, think it not too soon or too late to turn over the leaves of thy past life; and be sure to fold down where any passage of it may affect thee; and bestow thy remainder of time, to correct those faults in thy future conduct. Be it in relation to this or to the next life. What thou wouldst do, if what thou hast done were to go again, be sure to do as long as thou livest, upon the like occasions.

Frugality is good if liberality be joined with it. The first is leaving off superfluous expense; the last bestowing them to the benefit of others that need. The first without the last begins covetousness; the last without the first begins prodigality. Both together make an excellent temper. Happy the place where that is found.

If thou wouldst be happy and easy in thy family, above all things observe discipline.

Temperance – to this a spare diet contributes much. Eat therefore to live but do not live to eat. That's like a man, but this below a beast.

Excess in *apparel* is another costly folly. The very trimming of the vain world would clothe all the naked one.

Never marry but for love; but see that thou lov'st what is lovely.

But in marriage do thou be wise; prefer the person before money; virtue before beauty; the mind before the body; then thou hast a wife, a friend, a companion, a second self; one that bears an equal share with thee, in all thy toils and troubles.

If thou hast done an injury to another, rather own it, than defend it. One way thou gainest forgiveness, the other thou *doublest* the wrong and reckoning.

Do good with what thou hast, or it will do thee no good.

Seek not to be rich, but happy. The one lies in bags, the other in content; which wealth can never give.

If thou wouldst be happy, bring thy mind to thy condition, and have an indifferency for more than what is sufficient.

Be rather bountiful than expensive.

Neither make nor go to feasts, but let the laborious poor bless thee at home in their solitary cottages.

If thou thinkest twice before thou speakest once, thou wilt speak twice the better for it.

Nothing does reason more right than the *coolness* of those that offer it; for the truth often suffers more by the heat of its defenders, than from the arguments of its opposers.

Inquiry is human; blind obedience, brutal. Truth never loses by the one, but often suffers by the other.

Rarely promise. But, if lawful *constantly* perform.

Passion – It is the difference between a wise and a weak man; this judges by the lump, that by parts and their connection.

It is too common an error, to invert the order of things; by making an end of that which is a means, and a means of that which is an end.

Religion and government escape not this mischief; the first is too often made a means instead of an end; the other an end instead of a means.

If we are sure the end is right, we are too apt to gallop over all bounds to compass it; not considering that lawful ends may be very unlawfully attained.

Let us be careful to take just ways to compass just things; that they may last in their benefits to us.

Clean hands – let men have sufficient salaries, and exceed them at their peril.

If thou has not conquered thyself in that which is thy own particular weakness, thou has not title to virtue, though thou art free of other men's.

'Tis no sin to be tempted, but to be overcome …

Love is the hardest lesson in Christianity; but for that reason, it should be most our care to learn it.

He that judges not well of the importance of his affairs, though he may be always busy, he must make but small progress.

But make not more business necessary than is so; and rather lessen than augment work for thyself.

From *The Fruits of Solitude* by William Penn, 1693

39

NINE SPIRITUAL REMEDIES

1. A little more patience – to tolerate those with whom I must live and who are not at all congenial to me.
2. A little more perseverance – to continue this work which duty demands but which is repellent to me.
3. A little more humility – to remain at the post to which God has led me but which does not correspond with my dreams and plans.
4. A little more common sense – to take people as they are, not as I should like them to be.
5. A little more prudence – not to bother so much about other people's own business.
6. A little more strength – to endure that which so suddenly disturbs the soul.
7. A little more cheerfulness – so as not to show I have been hurt.
8. A little mor e unselfishness – in trying to understand the thoughts and feelings of others.
9. Above all, a little more prayer, to draw God to my heart and take counsel with him.

Author unknown

40

TWELVE WAYS TO BE HAPPY

1. Make up your mind to be happy. Learn to find pleasure in simple things.
2. Make the best of your circumstances. No one has everything and everyone has something of sorrow intermingled with the gladness of life. The trick is to make the laughter outweigh the tears.
3. Don't take yourself too seriously. Don't think that somehow you should be protected from misfortunes that befall others.
4. You can't please everyone. Don't let criticism worry you.
5. Don't let your neighbour set your standards. Be yourself.
6. Do the things you enjoy doing, but stay out of debt.
7. Don't borrow trouble. Imaginary things are harder to bear than the actual ones.
8. Since hate poisons the soul, do not cherish enmities, grudges. Avoid people who make you unhappy.
9. Have many interests. If you can't travel, read about new places.
10. Don't hold post-mortems. Don't spend your life brooding over sorrows and mistakes. Don't be the one who never gets over things.

11. Do what you can for those less fortunate than yourself.
12. Keep busy at something. A very busy person never has time to be unhappy.

From A *Pattern for Living* by Robert Louis Stevenson

41

THE TWELVE STEPS OF ALCOHOLICS ANONYMOUS

1. We admitted we were powerless over alcohol – that our lives had become unmanageable.
2. Came to believe that a Power greater than ourselves could restore us to sanity.
3. Made a decision to turn our will and our lives over to the care of God *as we understood Him*.
4. Made a searching and fearless moral inventory of ourselves.
5. Admitted to God, to ourselves, and to another human being the exact nature of our wrongs.
6. Were entirely ready to have God remove all these defects of character.
7. Humbly asked Him to remove our shortcomings.
8. Made a list of all persons we had harmed, and became willing to make amends to them all.

9. Made direct amends to such people wherever possible, except when to do so would injure them or others.
10. Continued to take personal inventory and when we were wrong promptly admitted it.
11. Sought through prayer and meditation to improve our conscious contact with God *as we understood Him*, praying only for knowledge of His will for us and the power to carry that out.
12. Having had a spiritual awakening as the result of these steps, we tried to carry this message to alcoholics, and to practise these principles in all our affairs.

From the book, *Alcoholics Anonymous*, 1939

42

GO PLACIDLY AMID THE NOISE AND HASTE

Go placidly amid the noise & haste, & remember what peace there may be in silence. As far as possible, without surrender, be on good terms with all persons. Speak your truth quietly & clearly; and listen to others, even the dull & ignorant: they too have their story.

Avoid loud & aggressive persons, they are vexatious to the spirit. If you compare yourself with others, you may become bitter or vain, for always there will be greater & lesser persons than yourself. Enjoy your achievements as well as your plans.

Keep interested in your own career, however humble; it is a real possession in the changing fortunes of time. Exercise caution in your business affairs; for the world is full of trickery. But let this not blind you to what virtue there is; many persons strive for high ideals; and everywhere life is full of heroism.

Be yourself. Especially, do not feign affection. Neither be cynical about love, for in the face of all aridity & disenchantment it is perennial as the grass.

Take kindly the counsel of the years, gracefully surrendering the things of youth. Nurture strength of spirit to shield you in sudden misfortune. But do not distress yourself with imaginings. Many fears are born of fatigue & loneliness. Beyond a wholesome discipline, be gentle with yourself.

You are a child of the universe, no less than the trees & the stars; you have a right to be here. And whether or not it is clear to you, no doubt the universe is unfolding as it should.

Therefore be at peace with God, whatever you conceive Him to be, and whatever your labors & aspirations, in the noisy confusion of life, keep peace with your soul.

With all its sham, drudgery & broken dreams, it is still a beautiful world. Be cheerful. Strive to be happy.

'Desiderata' by Max Ehrmann

43

MAKE FULL USE OF THIS LIFE

To get a human body is a rare thing. Make full use of it. There are four million kinds of lives which a soul can gather. After that, one gets a chance to be human, to get a human body. Therefore one should not waste this chance.

Every second in human life is very valuable. If you don't value this, then you will have nothing in hand and you will weep in the end.

Because you are human, God has given you power to think and decide what is good and bad. Therefore you can do the best possible kind of action.

You should never consider yourself a weak or fallen creature. Whatever may have happened up to now may be because you didn't know, but now, be careful ...

After getting a human body, if you do not reach God, you will have sold a diamond at the price of spinach.

From a talk by His Divinity Swami Brahmananda Saraswati

44

BEING TRUE TO SELF

What I must do is all that concerns me, not what the people think. This rule equally arduous in actual and in intellectual life, may serve for the whole distinction between greatness and meanness. It is the harder, because you will always find those who think they know what is your duty better than you know it. It is easy in the world to live after the world's opinion; it is easy in solitude to live after our own; but the great man is he who in the midst of the crowd keeps with perfect sweetness the independence of solitude.

The objection to conforming to usages that have become dead to you is, that it scatters your force. It loses your time and blurs the impression of your character ...

For non-conformity the world whips you with its displeasure. And therefore a man must know how to estimate a sour face. The bystanders look askance on him in the public street or in the friend's parlour. If this aversation had its origin in contempt and resistance like his own, he might well go home with a sad countenance: but the sour faces of the multitude, like their sweet faces, have no deep cause, but are put on and off as the wind blows and a newspaper directs ...

The other terror that scares us from self-trust is our consistency; a reverence for our past act or word, because the eyes of others have no other data for computing our orbit than our past acts, and we are loath to disappoint them.

But why should you keep your head over your shoulder? Why drag about this corpse of your memory, lest you contradict somewhat you have stated in this or that public place? Suppose you should contradict yourself; what then? It seems to be a rule of wisdom never to rely on your memory alone, scarcely even in acts of pure memory, but to bring the past for judgment into the thousand-eyed present, and live ever in a new day …

I hope in these days we have heard the last of conformity and consistency. Let the words be gazetted and ridiculous henceforward. Instead of the gong for dinner, let us hear a whistle from the Spartan fife. Let us never bow and apologise any more …

The relations of the soul to the divine spirit are so pure, that it is profane to seek to interpose helps. It must be that when God speaketh he should communicate not one thing, but all things; should fill the world with his voice; should scatter forth light, nature, time, souls, from the centre of the present thought; and new date and new create the whole. Whenever a mind is simple, and receives a divine wisdom, old things pass away – means, teachers, texts, temples fall; it lives now, and absorbs past and future into the present hour. All things are made sacred by relation to it – one as much as another. All things are dissolved to their centre by the cause, and, in the universal miracle, pretty and particular miracles disappear. If, therefore, a man claims to know and speak of

God, and carries you backward to the phraseology of some old mouldered nation in another country, in another world, believe him not. Is the acorn better than the oak which is its fullness and completion? Is the parent better than the child into whom he has cast his ripened being? Whence, then, this worship of the past? The centuries are conspirators against the sanity and authority of the soul. Time and space are but physiological colours which the eye makes, but the soul is light; where it is, is day; where it was, is night; and history is an impertinence and an injury, if it be anything more than a cheerful apologue or parable of my being and becoming.

Man is timid and apologetic; he is no longer upright; but he dares not say 'I think', 'I am', but quotes some saint or sage. He is ashamed before the blade of grass or the blowing rose. These roses under my window make no reference to former roses or to better ones; they are for what they are; they exist with God today. There is no time to them. There is simply the rose; it is perfect in every moment of its existence. Before a leaf-bud has burst, its whole life acts; in the full-blown flower there is no more; in the leafless root there is no less. Its nature is satisfied, and it satisfies nature, in all its moments alike. But man postpones or remembers; he does not live in the present, but with reverted eye laments the past, or, heedless of the riches that surround him, stands on tiptoe to foresee the future. He cannot be happy and strong until he too lives with nature in the present, above time.

From *Self Reliance* by Ralph Waldo Emerson, 1841

45

KRISHNA TELLS ARJUNA HOW TO WORK

Sri Krishna

You have the right to work, but never to the fruit of work. You should never engage in action for the sake of reward, nor should you long for inaction. Perform works in this world, Arjuna, as a man established within himself – without selfish attachments, and alike in success and defeat. For yoga (wisdom) is perfect evenness of mind.

Seek refuge in the attitude of detachment and you will amass the wealth of spiritual awareness. Those who are motivated only by desire for the fruits of action are miserable, for they are constantly anxious about the results of what they do. When consciousness is unified, however, all vain anxiety is left behind. There is no cause for worry, whether things go well or ill. Therefore devote yourself to the disciplines of yoga (wisdom), for yoga is skill in action.

The 'Bhagavad-Gita', 2, 47–50

46
THE DIVINISATION OF OUR ACTIVITIES

I do not think I am exaggerating when I say that nine out of ten practising Christians feel that a man's work is always at the level of a 'spiritual encumbrance'. In spite of the practice of right intentions, and the day offered every morning to God, the general run of the faithful dimly feel that time spent at the office or the studio, in the fields or in the factory, is time diverted from prayer and adoration. It is impossible not to work – that is taken for granted. But it is impossible, too, to aim at the deep religious life reserved for those who have the leisure to pray or preach all day long. A few moments of the day can be salvaged for God, yes, but the best hours are absorbed, or at any rate cheapened, by material cares ...

There are, of course, certain noble and cherished moments of the day, – those when we pray or receive the sacraments. But for these moments of more efficient or more explicit contact, the tide of the divine omnipresence, and our perception of it, would weaken until all that was best in our human endeavour, without being entirely lost to the world, would be for us emptied of God. But once we have jealously safeguarded our relation to God encountered, if I may dare use the expression, 'in a pure state' (that is to say in a state of being distinct from all the elements of this world), there is no need to fear that the most banal, absorbing or attractive of occupations should force us to depart from Him. To repeat: by virtue of the creation and still more, of the Incarnation, *nothing* here below *is profane* for those who know how to see. On the contrary, everything is sacred to those capable of distinguishing that portion of chosen being which is subject to the attraction of Christ in the process of consummation. Try, with God's help, to perceive the connection – even physical and natural – which binds your labour with the building of the Kingdom of Heaven; try to realise that heaven itself smiles upon you and, through your works, draws you to itself; then, as you leave church for the noisy streets, you will remain with only one feeling, that of continuing to immerse yourself in God. If your work is dull or exhausting take refuge in the inexhaustible and becalming interest of progressing in the divine life. If your work enthrals you, then allow the spiritual impulse which matter communicates to you to enter into your taste for God whom you know better and desire more under the veil of His works. Never, at any time, 'whether eating or drinking', consent to do anything without first of all realising its significance and constructive value *in Christo Jesu*, and pursuing it with all your might. This is not simply a commonplace precept for salvation: it is the very path to sanctity for each man according to his state and calling. For what sanctity in a creature if not to cleave to God with the maximum of his strength? And what does that maximum cleaving to God mean if not the fulfilment – in the world organised around Christ – of the exact function, be it lowly or eminent, to which that creature is destined both by nature and by supernature?

Within the Church we observe all sorts of groups whose members are vowed to the perfect practice or this and that particular virtue: mercy, detachment, the splendour of the liturgy, the missions, contemplation. Why should there not be men bowed to the task of exemplifying, by their lives, the general sanctification of human endeavour? – men whose common religious ideal would be to give a full and conscious explanation of the divine possibilities of demands which any worldly occupation implies – men, in a word, who would devote themselves, in the fields of thought, art, industry, commerce and politics, etc., to carrying out, in the sublime spirit these demand, the basic tasks which form the very bonework of human society? Around us the 'natural' progress which nourishes the sanctity of each new age is all too often left to the children of the world, that is to say to agnostics or the irreligious. Unconsciously or involuntarily, no doubt, these collaborate in the Kingdom of God and in the fulfilment of the elect; their efforts, transcending or correcting their incomplete or bad intentions, are gathered in by Him 'whose energy subjects all things to itself'. But that is no more than a second best, a temporary phase in the organisation of human activity. Right from the hands that knead the dough, to those that consecrate it, the great and universal Host should be prepared and handled in a spirit of *adoration*.

May the time come when men, having been awakened to a sense of the close bond linking all the movements of this world in the unique work of the Incarnation, shall be unable to give themselves to a single one of their tasks without illuminating it with the clear vision that their work – however elementary it may be – is received and made use of by a Centre of the universe.

When that comes to pass, there will be little to separate life in the cloister from the life of the world.

From *The Divine Milieu* by Pierre Teilhard de Chardin, 1960

47

TIME AND SIMPLICITY

Still we live meanly as ants; though the fable tells us that we were long ago changed into men; like pygmies we fight with cranes; it is error upon error, and clout upon clout, and our best virtue has for its occasion a superfluous and evitable wretchedness. Our life is frittered away by detail. An honest man has hardly need to count more than his ten fingers, or in extreme cases he may add his ten toes, and lump the rest. Simplicity, simplicity, simplicity! I say, let your affairs be as two or three, and not a hundred or a thousand; instead of a million count half-a-dozen, and keep your accounts on your thumbnail. In the midst of this chopping sea of civilised life, such are the clouds and storms and quick sands and thousand-and-one items to be allowed for, that a man has to live, if he would not founder and go to the bottom and not make his port at all, by dead reckoning, and he must be a great calculator indeed who succeeds. Simplify, simplify. Instead of three meals a-day, if it be necessary eat but one; instead of a hundred dishes, five; and reduce other things in proportion …

Let us spend one day as deliberately as Nature, and not be thrown off the track by every nutshell and mosquito's wing that falls on the rails. Let us rise early and fast, or break fast, gently and without perturbation; let company come and let company go, let the bells ring and the children cry, – determined to make a day of it. Why should we knock under and go with the stream? Let us not be upset and overwhelmed in that terrible rapid and whirlpool, called a dinner, situated in the meridian shallows. Weather this danger and you are safe, for the rest of the way is down hill. With unrelaxed nerves, with morning vigour, sail by it, looking another way, tied to the mast like Ulysses. If the engine whistles, let it whistle till it is hoarse for its pains. If the bell rings, why should we run? We will consider what kind of music they are like. Let us settle ourselves, and work and wedge our feet downward through the mud and slush of opinion, and prejudice, and tradition, and delusion, and appearance, that alluvion which covers the globe, through Paris and London, through New York and Boston and Concord, through church and state, through poetry and philosophy and religion, till we come to a hard bottom and rocks in place, which we can call *reality*, and say This is, and no mistake; and then begin, having a *point d'appui*, below freshet and frost and fire, a place where you might found a wall or a state, or set a lamp-post safely, or perhaps a gauge, not a Nilometer, but a Realometer, that future ages might know how deep a freshet of shams and appearances had gathered from time to time. If you stand right fronting and face to face to a fact, you will see the sun glimmer on both its surfaces, as if it were a cimeter, and feel its sweet edge dividing you through the heart and marrow, and so you will happily conclude your mortal career. Be it life or death, we crave only reality. If we are really dying, let us hear the rattle in our throats and feel cold in the extremities; if we are alive, let us go about our business.

Time is but the stream I go a-fishing in. I drink at it; but while I drink I see the sandy bottom and detect how shallow it is. Its thin current slides away, but eternity remains. I would drink deeper; fish in the sky, whose bottom is pebbly with stars. I cannot count one. I know not the first letter of the alphabet. I have always been regretting that I was not as wise as the day I was born. The intellect is a cleaver; it discerns and rifts its way into the secret of things. I do not wish to be any more busy with my hands than is necessary. My head is hands and feet. I feel all my best faculties concentrated in it. My instinct tells me that my head is an organ for burrowing, as some creatures use their snout and fore-paws, and with it I would mine and burrow my way through these hills. I think that the richest vein is somewhere hereabouts; so by the divining rod and thin rising vapours I judge; and here I will begin to mine.

From *Walden or Life in the Woods* by Henry David Thoreau, 1854

CHAPTER FOUR

LOVING, FORGIVING AND ACCEPTING OTHERS

I START WITH ST PAUL'S GLORIOUS passage about love, called here 'charity'. This love is not the romantic kind but the altruistic caring kind. Most of our major religions focus on the need to love others and to lead generous and forgiving lives. The Christian charity is the Buddhist compassion, for instance. There are differences in emphasis but roughly the same theme. And if we want to love and forgive others, we must give up judging them, knowing what is best for them, helping them when they don't want help, controlling or intervening in their lives. I find this difficult.

48

A DEFINITION OF UNCONDITIONAL LOVE

Though I speak with the tongues of men and of angels, and have not charity, I am become as sounding brass, or a tinkling cymbal.

And though I have the gift of prophecy, and understand all mysteries, and all knowledge; and though I have all faith, so that I could remove mountains, and have not charity, I am nothing.

And though I bestow all my goods to feed the poor, and though I give my body to be burned, and have not charity, it profiteth me nothing.

Charity suffereth long, and is kind; charity envieth not; charity vaunteth not itself, is not puffed up,

Doth not behave itself unseemly, seeketh not her own, is not easily provoked, thinketh no evil;

Rejoiceth not in iniquity, but rejoiceth in the truth;

Beareth all things, believeth all things, hopeth all things, endureth all things.

Charity never faileth: but whether there be prophecies, they shall fail; whether there be tongues, they shall cease; whether there be knowledge, it shall vanish away.

For we know in part, and we prophesy in part.

But when that which is perfect is come, then that which is in part shall be done away.

When I was a child, I spake as a child, I understood as a child, I thought as a child: but when I became a man, I put away childish things.

For now we see through a glass, darkly; but then face to face: now I know in part; but then shall I know even as also I am known.

And now abideth faith, hope, charity, these three; but the greatest of these is charity.

St Paul's First Epistle to the Corinthians 13:1–13

49

LOVING YOUR NEIGHBOUR IN JUDAISM

Thou shalt not avenge, nor bear any grudge against the children of thy people, but thou shalt love thy neighbour as thyself: I am the LORD …

And if a stranger sojourn with thee in your land, ye shall not vex him.

But the stranger that dwelleth with you shall be unto you as one born among you, and thou shalt love him as thyself; for ye were strangers in the land of Egypt: I am the LORD your God.

Leviticus 19:18, 33–4.

50
WHO IS MY NEIGHBOUR?

And, behold, a certain lawyer stood up, and tempted him [Jesus], saying, Master, what shall I do to inherit eternal life?

He said unto him, What is written in the law? how readest thou?

And he answering said, Thou shalt love the Lord thy God with all thy heart, and with all thy soul, and with all thy strength, and with all thy mind; and thy neighbour as thyself.

And he said unto him, Thou hast answered right: this do, and thou shalt live.

But he, willing to justify himself, said unto Jesus, And who is my neighbour?

And Jesus answering said, A certain man went down from Jerusalem to Jericho, and fell among thieves, which stripped him of his raiment, and wounded him, and departed, leaving him half dead.

And by chance there came down a certain priest that way: and when he saw him, he passed by on the other side.

And likewise a Levite, when he was at the place, came and looked on him, and passed by on the other side.

But a certain Samaritan, as he journeyed, came where he was: and when he saw him, he had compassion on him,

And went to him, and bound up his wounds, pouring in oil and wine, and set him on his own beast, and brought him to an inn, and took care of him.

And on the morrow when he departed, he took out two pence, and gave them to the host, and said unto him, Take care of him; and whatsoever thou spendest more, when I come again, I will repay thee.

Which now of these three, thinkest thou, was neighbour unto him that fell among the thieves?

And he said, He that shewed mercy on him. Then said Jesus unto him, Go, and do thou likewise.

The Gospel of St Luke 10:25–37

51

JESUS ON THE ULTIMATE PROOF OF LOVE

This passage is part of a series of sayings by Jesus Christ, in response to questions from his disciples.

As the Father hath loved me, so have I loved you: continue ye in my love.

If ye keep my commandments, ye shall abide in my love; even as I have kept my Father's commandments, and abide in his love.

These things have I spoken unto you, that my joy might remain in you, and that your joy might be full.
This is my commandment, That ye love one another, as I have loved you.
Greater love hath no man than this, that a man lay down his life for his friends.

The Gospel of St John 15:9–17

52

LOVE YOUR NEIGHBOUR IN ISLAM

God will say on the Day of Resurrection: O son of Adam, I fell ill and you visited Me not. He will say: O Lord, and how should I visit You when You are the Lord of the universe? God will say: Did you not know that My servant So-and-so had fallen ill and you visited him not? Did you not know that had you visited him you would have found Me with him? O son of Adam, I asked you for food and you fed Me not. He will say: O Lord, and how should I feed You when You are the Lord of the universe? God will say: Did you not know that My servant So-and-so asked you for food and you fed him not? Did you not know that had you fed him you would surely have found that [the reward for doing so] with Me? O son of Adam, I asked you to give Me to drink and you gave Me not to drink. He will say: O Lord, how should I give You to drink when You are the Lord of the universe? God will say: My servant So-and-so asked you to give him to drink and you gave him not to drink. Had you given him to drink you would have surely found that with Me.

One of the *Hadith*, the collection of the Prophet Muhammad's sayings.

53

LOVING YOUR NEIGHBOUR IN PRACTICE

Do all the good you can,
By all the means you can,
In all the ways you can,
In all the places you can,
At all the times you can,
To all the people you can,
As long as ever you can.

John Wesley, eighteenth century

54

THE BUDDHA'S SERMON ON RETURNING GOOD FOR EVIL

And the Blessed One observed the ways of society and noticed how much misery came from malignity and foolish offences done only to gratify vanity and self-seeking pride.

And the Buddha said: 'If a man foolishly does me wrong, I will return to him the protection of my ungrudging love; the more evil comes from him, the more good shall go from me; the fragrance of goodness always comes to me, and the harmful air of evil goes to him.'

A foolish man learning that the Buddha observed the principle of great love which commends the return of good for evil, came and abused him. The Buddha was silent, pitying his folly.

When the man had finished his abuse, the Buddha asked him, saying: 'Son, if a man declined to accept a present made to him, to whom would it belong?' And he answered; 'In that case it would belong to the man who offered it.'

'My son,' said the Buddha, 'thou hast railed at me, but I decline to accept thy abuse, and request thee to keep it thyself. Will it not be a source of misery to thee? As the echo belongs to the sound, and the shadow to the substance, so misery will overtake the evil-doer without fail.'

The abuser made no reply, and the Buddha continued:

'A wicked man who reproaches a virtuous one is like one who looks up and spits at heaven; the spittle soils not the heaven, but comes back and defiles his own person.

'The slanderer is like one who flings dust at another when the wind is contrary; the dust does but return on him who threw it. The virtuous man cannot be hurt and the misery that the other would inflict comes back on himself.'

The abuser went away ashamed, but he came again and took refuge in the Buddha, the Dharma [the path of Buddhist teachings] and the Sangha [the Buddhist church].

From the *Sutra of Forty-Two Sections*, c.67

55

GOD'S LOVE AND FORGIVENESS

Then drew near unto him [Jesus] all the publicans and sinners for to hear him.

And the Pharisees and scribes murmured, saying, This man receiveth sinners, and eateth with them.

And he spake this parable unto them, saying,

What man of you, having an hundred sheep, if he lose one of them, doth not leave the ninety and nine in the wilderness, and go after that which is lost, until he find it?

And when he hath found it, he layeth it on his shoulders, rejoicing.
And when he cometh home, he calleth together his friends and neighbours, saying unto them, Rejoice with me; for I have found my sheep which was lost.
I say unto you, that likewise joy shall be in heaven over one sinner that repenteth, more than over ninety and nine just persons, which need no repentance …
And he said, A certain man had two sons:
And the younger of them said to his father, Father, give me the portion of goods that falleth to me. And he divided unto them his living.
And not many days after the younger son gathered all together, and took his journey into a far country, and there wasted his substance with riotous living.
And when he had spent all, there arose a mighty famine in that land; and he began to be in want.
And he went and joined himself to a citizen of that country; and he sent him into his fields to feed swine.
And he would fain have filled his belly with the husks that the swine did eat: and no man gave unto him.
And when he came to himself, he said, How many hired servants of my father's have bread enough and to spare, and I perish with hunger!
I will arise and go to my father, and will say unto him, Father, I have sinned against heaven, and before thee,
And am no more worthy to be called thy son: make me as one of thy hired servants.

And he arose, and came to his father. But when he was yet a great way off, his father saw him, and had compassion, and ran, and fell on his neck, and kissed him.

And the son said unto him, Father, I have sinned against heaven, and in thy sight, and am no more worthy to be called thy son.

But the father said to his servants, Bring forth the best robe, and put it on him; and put a ring on his hand, and shoes on his feet:

And bring hither the fatted calf, and kill it; and let us eat, and be merry:

For this my son was dead, and is alive again; he was lost, and is found. And they began to be merry.

Now his elder son was in the field: and as he came and drew nigh to the house, he heard musick and dancing.

And he called one of the servants, and asked what these things meant.

And he said unto him, Thy brother is come; and thy father hath killed the fatted calf, because he hath received him safe and sound.

And he was angry, and would not go in: therefore came his father out, and intreated him.

And he answering said to his father, Lo, these many years do I serve thee, neither transgressed I at any time thy commandment: and yet thou never gavest me a kid, that I might make merry with my friends:

But as soon as this thy son was come, which hath devoured thy living with harlots, thou hast killed for him the fatted calf.

And he said unto him, Son, thou art ever with me, and all that I have is thine.

It was meet that we should make merry, and be glad: for this thy brother was dead, and is alive again; and was lost, and is found.

The Gospel of St Luke 15:1–7, 11–32

56

DR SAMUEL JOHNSON ON FORGIVING EARLY

No law of our Redeemer is more openly transgressed, or more industriously evaded, than that by which he commands his followers to forgive injuries, and prohibits, under the sanction of eternal misery, the gratification of that desire which every man feels of returning any pain that he suffers upon him that inflicts it. Many who could have conquered their anger are unable to combat against pride, and pursue offences to the extremity of vengeance, only lest they should be insulted by the triumph of an enemy.

But certainly no precept could better become him, at whose birth peace was proclaimed to the earth. For what would so soon destroy all the order of society, and deform life with violence and ravage, as a permission to every man to judge his own cause, and to apportion his own recompense for imagined injuries.

It is difficult for a man of the strictest justice not to favour himself too much in his calmest moments, or his solitary meditations. Every one wishes for distinctions and superiority, for which thousands are wishing at the same time, in their own opinion, with better claims. He that, when his reason operates in its full force, can thus, by the mere prevalence of self-love, prefer himself to his fellow beings, is not likely to judge equitably when his passions are agitated by a sense of wrong, and his attention wholly engrossed by his pain, his interest, or his danger. Whoever claims to himself the right of vengeance, shows how little he is qualified to judge his own cause, since he certainly demands what he would think unfit to be granted to another.

Nothing is more apparent than that, however injured or however provoked, some must at last be contented to forgive; for it can never be hoped, that he who commits an injury, will contentedly acquiesce in the penalty required. The same haughtiness of contempt, and vehemence of desire, that prompts the act of injustice, will more strongly incite its justification; and resentment can seldom so exactly balance the punishment with the fault, but there will remain an overplus of vengeance which even he who condemns his first action will think himself entitled to retaliate. What then can ensue but a continual exacerbation of hatred, an unextinguishable feud, an incessant reciprocation of mischief, a mutual vigilance to entrap, and effort to destroy.

Since the imaginary right of vengeance must be at last remitted, because it is impossible to live in perpetual hostility, and equally impossible that of two enemies, either should think himself obliged by justice to submission, it is surely eligible to forgive early. Every passion is more easily subdued before it has been accustomed to long possession of the heart; every idea is obliterated with less difficulty as it has been more slightly impressed, and less frequently renewed. He who has long brooded over his wrongs, pleased himself with schemes of malignity, and glutted his imagination with the joys of triumph, and supplications of humbled enmity, will not easily open his bosom to amity and reconciliation, or indulge the gentle sentiments of benevolence and peace.

It is easiest to forgive, while there is yet little to be forgiven. A single injury may be soon dismissed from the memory, but a long succession of ill offices by degrees associated itself with every idea, and a long contest will involve so many circumstances, that every place and every action will recall it to the mind, and fresh remembrance of vexation must still enkindle rage, and irritate revenge.

A wise man will make haste to forgive, because he who knows the true value of time will not suffer it to pass away in unnecessary pain. He that willingly suffers the corrosions of inveterate hatred, and gives up his days and nights to the gloom of malice and perturbations of stratagem, cannot surely be said to consult his ease. Resentment is union of sorrow with malignity, a combination of passion which all endeavour to avoid, with a passion which all concur to detest. The man who retires to mediate mischief, and to exasperate his own rage, whose thoughts are employed only on scenes of distress and contrivances of ruin, whose mind never pauses from the remembrance of his own sufferings, but to indulge some hope of enjoying the miseries of another, may justly be numbered among the most miserable of human beings, among those who are guilty without reward, who have neither the gladness of prosperity, nor the calm of innocence.

He that considers the weakness both of himself and others will not long want persuasives to forgiveness. We cannot know to what degree of malignity any injury is to be imputed, or how much its guilt, if we were to inspect the mind of him that committed it, would be extenuated by mistake, precipitance, or negligence; nor can we be always certain how much more we feel than was intended to be inflicted, or how much we increase the mischief to ourselves by voluntary aggravations. We may charge to design the effects of accidents, we may think the blow violent only because we have made ourselves delicate and tender, we are on every side in danger of error and of guilt, which we are certain to avoid only by speedy forgiveness.

From this pacific and harmless temper, thus propitious to others and ourselves, to domestic tranquillity and to social happiness, no man is withheld but by pride, by the fear of being insulted by his adversary or despised by the world.

It may be laid down as an unfailing and universal axiom, that, 'all pride is abject and mean'. It is always an ignorant, lazy, or cowardly acquiescence, in a false appearance of excellence, and proceeds not from consciousness of our attainments but insensibility of our wants.

Nothing can be great which is not right. Nothing which reason condemns can be suitable to the dignity of the human mind. To permit ourselves to be driven by external motives from the way which our own heart approves, to give way to any thing but conviction, to suffer the opinion of others to over-rule our choice or overpower our resolves, is to submit tamely to the lowest and most ignominious slavery, and to resign the right of directing our own lives …

Of him that hopes to be forgiven, it is indispensably required that he forgive; it is therefore superfluous to urge any other motive; on this great duty, eternity is suspended; and to him that refuses to practise it, the throne of mercy is inaccessible, and the Saviour of the World has been born in vain.

Dr Samuel Johnson, 1709–84

57

FORGIVENESS HEALS US

However much we have been wronged, however justified our hatred, if we cherish it, it will poison us. It is in forgiving our enemies that we are healed.

Dr Sheila Cassidy, doctor and psychotherapist, living

58

A SPIRIT THAT DELIGHTS TO DO NO EVIL

There is a spirit which I feel that delights to do no evil, nor to revenge any wrong, but delights to endure all things, in hope to enjoy its own in the end. Its hope is to outlive all wrath and contention, and to weary out all exaltation and cruelty, or whatever is of a nature contrary to itself. It sees the end of all temptations. As it bears no evil in itself, so it conceives none in thoughts to any other. If it be betrayed, it bears it, for its ground and spring is the mercies and forgiveness of God. Its crown is meekness, its life is everlasting love unfeigned; it takes its kingdom with entreaty and not with contention, and keeps it by lowliness of mind. In God alone, it can rejoice, though no-one else regard it, or can own its life. It's conceived in sorrow, and brought forth without any to pity it, nor doth it murmur at grief and oppression. It never rejoiceth but through sufferings; for with the world's joy it is murdered. I found it alone, being forsaken. I have fellowship therein with them who lived in dens and desolate places in the earth, who through death obtained this resurrection and eternal holy life.

The last words of James Nayler, Quaker, 1617–60

59

MAY I BE NO MAN'S ENEMY

May I be no man's enemy, and may I be the friend of that which is eternal and abides.

May I never quarrel with those nearest to me, and if I do, may I be reconciled quickly.

May I never devise evil against any man; if any devise evil against me, may I escape uninjured and without the need of hurting him.

May I love, seek, attain only that which is good.

May I wish for all men's happiness and envy none.

May I never rejoice in the ill-fortune of one that has wronged me...

When I have done or said what is wrong, may I never wait for the rebuke of others, but always rebuke myself until I make amends ...

May I win no victory that harms either me or my opponent ...

May I reconcile friends who are angry with one another.

May I, to the extent of my power, give all needful help to my friends and all who are in want.

May I never fail a friend who is in danger.

When visiting those in grief may I be able by gentle and healing words to soothe their pain ...

May I respect myself.

May I always keep tame that which rages within me …

May I accustom myself to be gentle, and never be angry with people because of circumstances.

May I never discuss who is wicked and what wicked things he has done, but know good men and follow in their footsteps.

Attributed to Eusebius, third to fourth century

60

OF BEARING WITH THE DEFECTS OF OTHERS

Those things that a man cannot amend in himself or in others, he ought to suffer patiently, until God order things otherwise.

Think that perhaps it is better so for thy trial and patience, without which all our good deeds are not much to be esteemed.

Thou oughtest to pray notwithstanding when thou hast such impediments, that God would vouchsafe to help thee, and that thou mayest bear them kindly.

If one that is once or twice warned will not give over, contend not with him: but commit all to God, that His will may be fulfilled, and His name honoured in all His servants, who well knoweth how to turn evil into good.

Endeavour to be patient in bearing with the defects and infirmities of others, of what sort so ever they be; for that thyself also hast many failings which must be borne with by others.

If thou canst not make thyself such a one as thou wouldest, how canst thou expect to have another in all things to thy liking?

We would willingly have others perfect, and yet we amend not our own faults.

We will have others severely corrected, and will not be corrected ourselves.

The large liberty of others displeaseth us; and yet we will not have our own desires denied us.

We will have others kept under by strict laws; but in no sort will ourselves be restrained.

And thus it appeareth, how seldom we weigh our neighbour in the same balance with ourselves.

If all men were perfect, what should we have to suffer of our neighbour for God?

But now God hath thus ordered it, that we may learn to bear one another's burdens; for no man is without fault; no man but hath his burden; no man sufficient of himself; no man wise enough of himself; but we ought to bear with one another, comfort one another, help, instruct, and admonish one another.

Occasions of adversity best discover how great virtue or strength each one hath. For occasions do not make a man frail, but they shew what he is.

St Thomas à Kempis, monk and writer, c.1379–1471

61

UNDERSTANDING OTHERS

The Bull Mountain was once covered with lovely trees. But it is near the capital of a great state. People came with their axes and choppers; they cut the woods down, and the mountain has lost its beauty. Yet even so, the day air and the night air came to it, rain and dew moistened it. Here and there fresh sprouts began to grow. But soon cattle and sheep came along and browsed on them, and in the end the mountain became gaunt and bare, as it is now. And seeing it thus gaunt and bare people imagine that it was woodless from the start. Now just as the natural state of the mountain was quite different from what now appears, so too in every man (little though they may be apparent) there assuredly were once feelings of decency and kindness; and if these good feelings are no longer there, it is that they have been tampered with, hewn down with axe and bill. As each day dawns they are assailed anew. What chance then has our nature, any more than that mountain, of keeping its beauty? To us too, as to the mountain, comes the air of day, the air of night. Just at dawn, indeed, we have for a moment and in a certain degree a mood in which our promptings and aversions come near to being such as are proper to men. But something is sure to happen before the morning is over, by which these better feelings are either checked or perhaps utterly destroyed. And in the end, when they have been checked again and again, the night air is no longer able to preserve them, and soon our feelings are as near as may be to those of beasts and birds; so that anyone might make the same mistake about us as about the mountain, and think there was never any good in us from the very start. Yet assuredly our present state of feeling is not what we began with. Truly,

> If rightly tended, no creature but thrives;
> If left untended, no creature but pines away.

Confucius said:

> Hold fast to it and you can keep it,
> Let go, and it will stray.
> For its comings and goings it has no time nor tide;
> None knows where it will bide.

Surely it was of the (innate good) feelings that he was speaking.

Mencius, fourth century BC

62

A PRAYER FOR TOLERATION

Father, who has made all men in thy likeness, and lovest all whom thou hast made, suffer not the world to separate itself from Thee by building barriers of race and colour. As thy Son, our Saviour, was born of a Hebrew mother, yet rejoiced in the faith of a Syrian woman and of a Roman soldier, welcomed the Greeks who sought him and suffered a man from Africa to carry his cross, so teach us to regard the members of all races as fellow-heirs of the kingdom of Jesus Christ, our Lord.

Oliver Warner for Toc H, twentieth century

63

ON LETTING GO RATHER THAN CONTROLLING

To let go does not mean to stop caring – it means I can't do it for someone else.

To let go is not to cut myself off – it's the realisation I can't control another.

To let go is not to enable – but to allow learning from natural consequences.

To let go is to admit powerlessness – which means the outcome is not in my hands.

To let go is not to try to change or blame another – it is to make the most of myself.

To let go is not to care for – but to care about.

To let go is not to fix somebody – but to be supportive to somebody.

To let go is not to judge – but to allow another to be a human being.

To let go is not to be in the middle arranging all the outcomes – but to allow others to affect their destinies.

To let go is not to be protective – it's to permit another to face reality.

To let go is not to deny – but to accept.

To let go is not to nag, scold or argue – but to search out my own shortcomings and correct them.

To let go is not to adjust everything to my own desires – but to take each day as it comes and cherish myself in it.

To let go is not to criticise and regulate anybody – but to try to become what I dream I can be.

To let go is not to regret the past – but to grow and live for the future.

To let go is to fear less – and to love more.

Author unknown

CHAPTER FIVE

DIFFICULTIES, DESPAIR AND GRACE

*A*T TIMES OF ANXIETY, GLOOM, *sorrow and despair, these are the passages that have helped me. Some were lifesavers for the times when I was confused, anxious, tempted to dishonesty or even in such emotional pain that I was close to self-destruction. Some of them can be used as a kind of mantra – reread over and over again, to block out the painful obsessions and despair in the mind. Some I have written down and carried about for several days to read at bad moments.*

64

WHAT TO DO WHEN IN A DIFFICULT POSITION

Give up money, give up fame, give up science, give the earth itself and all it contains, rather than do an immoral act. And never suppose, that in any possible situation, or under any circumstances, it is best for you to do a dishonourable thing, however slightly so it may appear to you. Whenever you are to do a thing, though it can never be known but to you, ask yourself how you would act were all the world looking at you, and act accordingly. Encourage all your virtuous dispositions, and exercise them whenever an opportunity arises; being assured that they will gain strength by exercise, as a limb of the body does, and that exercise will make them habitual. From the practice of the purest virtue, you may be assured you will derive the most sublime comforts in every moment of life, and in the moment of death. If ever you find yourself environed with difficulties and perplexing circumstances, out of which you are at a loss how to extricate yourself, do what is right, and be assured that that will extricate you the best out of the worst situations. Though you cannot see, when you take one step, what will be the next, yet follow truth, justice and plain dealing, and never fear their leading you out of the labyrinth, in the easiest manner possible. The knot which you thought a

Gordian one, will untie itself before you. Nothing is so mistaken as the supposition, that a person is to extricate himself from a difficulty, by intrigue, by chicanery, by dissimulation, by trimming, by an untruth, by an injustice. This increases the difficulties tenfold; and those, who pursue these methods, get themselves so involved at length, that they can turn no way but their infamy becomes more exposed. It is of great importance to set a resolution, not to be shaken, never to tell an untruth. There is no vice so mean, so pitiful, so contemptible; and he who permits himself to tell a lie once, finds it much easier to do it a second and third time, till at length it becomes habitual; he tells lies without attending to it, and truths without the world's believing him. This falsehood of the tongue leads to that of the heart, and in time depraves all its good dispositions.

From a letter by Thomas Jefferson, 19 August 1785

65

JESUS TALKS ABOUT POSSESSIONS AND ANXIETY

And he said unto them, Take heed, and beware of covetousness: for a man's life consisteth not in the abundance of the things which he possesseth.

And he spake a parable unto them, saying, The ground of a certain rich man brought forth plentifully:

And he thought within himself, saying, What shall I do, because I have no room where to bestow my fruits?

And he said, This will I do: I will pull down my barns, and build greater; and there will I bestow all my fruits and my goods.

And I will say to my soul, Soul, thou hast much goods laid up for many years; take thine ease, eat, drink, and be merry.

But God said unto him, Thou fool, this night thy soul shall be required of thee: then whose shall those things be, which thou hast provided?

So is he that layeth up treasure for himself, and is not rich toward God.

And he said unto his disciples, Therefore I say unto you, Take no thought for your life, what ye shall eat; neither for the body, what ye shall put on.

The life is more than meat, and the body is more than raiment.

Consider the ravens: for they neither sow nor reap; which neither have storehouse nor barn; and God feedeth them: how much more are ye better than the fowls?

And which of you with taking thought can add to his stature one cubit?

If ye then be not able to do that thing which is least, why take ye thought for the rest?

Consider the lilies how they grow: they toil not, they spin not; and yet I say unto you, that Solomon in all his glory was not arrayed like one of these.

If then God so clothe the grass, which is to day in the field,

and to morrow is cast into the oven; how much more will
he clothe you, O ye of little faith?
And seek not ye what ye shall eat, or what ye shall drink,
neither be ye of doubtful mind.
For all these things do the nations of the world seek after: and
your Father knoweth that ye have need of these things.
But rather seek ye the kingdom of God; and all these things
shall be added unto you.
Fear not, little flock; for it is your Father's good pleasure to
give you the kingdom.

The Gospel of St Luke 12:15–32

66

ANXIETY AND WORRY MAKE THINGS WORSE

Anxiety is not only a temptation of itself, but a conduit for many other temptations. I should therefore say something about it. This unhappiness is nothing other than the grief of mind that makes us suffer when, against our will, we face some trouble – whether that trouble is exterior like poverty, sickness, the contempt of others, or whether it is interior like ignorance, dryness of heart, repugnance or temptation. When the heart perceives this trouble, we become sad, unhappy, and with good reason extremely anxious to escape it; for everyone naturally desires what is good and avoids from what he thinks is bad.

If we want to be delivered for the love of God from this trouble, we will seek deliverance with patience, meekness, humility and tranquillity, looking for help from the goodness of God not from our own efforts or our own hard work. But if we seek deliverance out of self-love, we will exhaust ourselves seeking an escape, as if it depended more on ourselves than upon God. I do not say that we necessarily think this, but I say that we act as if we thought so.

Now, if we do not get what we want immediately, we become enormously anxious and impatient, and this does not overcome the trouble but rather makes it worse. We become anguished and distressed, our courage and strength fail us, so that it seems as if the trouble is beyond remedy. You see then that unhappiness, which is at first justifiable, leads to anxiety and the anxiety in turn increases the unhappiness, until it becomes extremely dangerous.

This anxiety is the greatest evil that can befall us, other than sin. For just as revolts and disturbances within a country ruin it entirely, and prevent it from being able to resist a foreign invasion, so we, when we are upset and anxious, lose the strength to maintain the virtues which we have acquired, and we lose the ability to resist the temptation of the enemy, who then makes all kinds of efforts to fish, as the saying goes, in troubled waters.

Anxiety proceeds from an inordinate desire to be delivered

from ill which we experience or to acquire some good which we hope for. And yet there is nothing which so aggravates trouble or removes the good further off, than anxiety and over-eagerness. Birds are ensnared in nets, because when they are caught, they flutter and struggle madly to escape, which makes them entangled even more. When therefore you are in a hurry to be delivered from some trouble or to obtain some good, above all make your mind restful and serene, and compose your judgment and your will. Then, quietly and gently, pursue what you desire, by whatever means are suitable. When I say 'quietly' I do not mean negligently, but without rashness, agitation and anxiety. Otherwise instead of achieving what you want, you will spoil everything and will get into more difficulties.

'My soul is continually in my hand, O Lord: yet do I not forget thy law' said David. Ask yourself more than once a day, but always at least in the evening and morning, whether you have your soul in your hands, or whether some passion or anxiety has taken possession of it; ask yourself whether your mind is under control, or whether it has escaped from you and is taken over by unruly love, hatred, envy, avarice, fear, worldly boredom, or joy. If it has escaped from your control, then immediately seek it out and bring it back quietly into the presence of God, putting your feelings and desires back into obedience to the divine will. Like people who are frightened of losing something which is precious to them and hold it rightly in their hand, so, in imitation of that great king, David, we must always say: 'O my God, my soul is in danger, and therefore I carry it always in my hand, and in this manner I have not forgotten thy holy law.'

Do not let your desires, however trivial and unimportant, make you anxious for if you do so, the bigger and more important ones will find your heart already troubled and disordered. When you suffer from anxiety, turn to God and resolve to take no action until your anxiety has entirely gone, unless it involves something that cannot be put off. In this case you must gently and serenely try to restrain your desire, moderating your feelings as much as possible, and then taking action according to reason, not according to your inclination.

If you can express your feelings of anxiety to your spiritual director, or at least to some good and faithful friend, be assured that you will feel better. For to reveal the sufferings of the heart has the same effect on the soul, as blood-letting helps those who have a chronic fever. It is the best remedy of all. As the king, St Louis, advised his son: 'If any trouble affects you, tell it to your confessor or to another good person, and the comfort he will give you will enable you to bear it easily.'

From a letter of St Francis de Sales, seventeenth century

67

THE LORD COMFORTS HIS PEOPLE

But now thus saith the LORD that created thee, O Jacob, and he that formed thee, O Israel, Fear not: for I have redeemed thee, I have called thee by thy name; thou art mine.

When thou passest through the waters, I will be with thee; and through the rivers, they shall not overflow thee: when thou walkest through the fire, thou shalt not be burned; neither shall the flame kindle upon thee.

For I am the LORD thy God, the Holy One of Israel, thy Saviour: I gave Egypt for thy ransom, Ethiopia and Seba for thee.

Since thou wast precious in my sight, thou hast been honourable, and I have loved thee: therefore will I give men for thee, and people for thy life.

Fear not: for I am with thee: I will bring thy seed from the east, and gather thee from the west;

I will say to the north, Give up; and to the south, Keep not back: bring my sons from far, and my daughters from the ends of the earth;

Even every one that is called by my name: for I have created him for my glory, I have formed him; yea, I have made him.

Bring forth the blind people that have eyes, and the deaf that have ears.

Let all the nations be gathered together, and let the people be assembled: who among them can declare this, and shew us former things? let them bring forth their witnesses, that they may be justified: or let them hear, and say, It is truth.

Ye are my witnesses, saith the LORD, and my servant whom I have chosen: that ye may know and believe me, and understand that I am he: before me there was no God formed, neither shall there be after me.

I, even I, am the LORD; and beside me there is no saviour.

I have declared, and have saved, and I have shewed, when there was no strange god among you: therefore ye are my witnesses, saith the LORD, that I am God.

Yea, before the day was I am he; and there is none that can deliver out of my hand: I will work, and who shall let it?

Thus saith the LORD, your redeemer, the Holy One of Israel; For your sake I have sent to Babylon, and have brought down all their nobles, and the Chaldeans, whose cry is in the ships.

I am the LORD, your Holy One, the creator of Israel, your King.

Thus saith the LORD, which maketh a way in the sea, and a path in the mighty waters;

Which bringeth forth the chariot and horse, the army and the power; they shall lie down together, they shall not rise: they are extinct, they are quenched as tow.

Remember ye not the former things, neither consider the things of old.

Behold, I will do a new thing; now it shall spring forth; shall ye not know it? I will even make a way in the wilderness, and rivers in the desert.

The beast of the field shall honour me, the dragons and the owls: because I give waters in the wilderness, and rivers in the desert, to give drink to my people, my chosen.

Isaiah 43:1–20

68

EVILS WE INFLICT ON OURSELVES

Men frequently think that the evils in the world are more numerous than the good things; many sayings and songs of the nations dwell on this idea. They say that the good is found only exceptionally, whilst evil things are numerous and lasting. The origin of this error is to be found in the circumstance that men judge of the whole universe by examining one single person only. If anything happens to him contrary to his expectation, of the which they conclude that the whole universe is evil. All mankind at present in existence form only an infinitesimal portion of the permanent universe. It is of great advantage that man should know his station. Numerous evils to which persons are exposed are due to the defects existing in the persons themselves. We seek relief from our own faults; we suffer from evils which we inflict on ourselves, and we ascribe them to God, Who is far from connected with them. As Solomon explained it: 'The foolishness of man perverted his way, and his heart fretteth against the Lord.'

Moses Maimonides, twelfth century

69

ENDURE ABUSE LIKE THE ELEPHANT

Silently shall I endure abuse as the elephant in battle endures the arrow sent from the bow: for the world is ill-natured.

A tamed elephant they lead to battle, the king mounts a tamed elephant; the tamed is the best among men, he who silently endures abuse.

Mules are good, if tamed, and noble Sindhu horses, and elephants with large tusks; but he who tames himself is better still.

For with these animals does no man reach the untrodden country [Nirvana], where a tamed man goes on a tamed animal, viz. on his own well-tamed self.

The elephant called Dhamapalaka, his temples running with sap, and difficult to hold, does not eat a morsel when bound; the elephant longs for the elephant grove.

If a man becomes fat and a great eater, if he is sleepy and rolls himself about, that fool, like a hog fed on wash, is born again and again.

This mind of mine went formerly wandering about as it liked, as it listed, as it pleased; but I shall now hold it in thoroughly, as the rider who holds the hook holds in the furious elephant.

Be not thoughtless, watch your thoughts! Draw yourself out of the evil way, like an elephant sunk in mud.

If a man finds a prudent companion who walks with him, is wise, and lives soberly, he may walk with him overcoming all dangers, happy, but considerate.

If a man find not prudent companion who walks with him, is wise, and lives soberly, let him walk alone, like a king who has left his conquered country behind – like a lonely elephant.

It is better to live alone, there is no companionship with a fool; let a man walk alone, let him commit no sin, with few wishes, like the lonely elephant.

If an occasion arises, friends are pleasant; enjoyment is pleasant if it is mutual; a good work is pleasant in the house of death; the giving up of all grief is pleasant.

The Dhammapada 23, 320–31

70

THE AS IF PRINCIPLE

There is, accordingly, no better known or more generally useful precept in the moral training of youth, or in one's personal self-discipline, than that which bids us pay primary attention to what we do and express, and not to care too much for what we feel. If we only check a cowardly impulse in time, for example, or if we only *don't* strike the blow or rip out with the complaining or insulting word that we shall regret as long as we live, our feelings themselves will presently be the calmer and better, with no particular guidance from us on their own account. Action seems to follow feeling, but really action and feeling go together; and by regulating the action, which is under the more direct control of the will, we can indirectly regulate the feeling, which is not.

Thus the sovereign voluntary path to cheerfulness, if our spontaneous cheerfulness be lost, is to sit up cheerfully, to look round cheerfully, and to act and speak as if cheerfulness were already there. If such conduct does not make you soon feel cheerful, nothing else on that occasion can. So to feel brave, act as if we *were* brave, use all our will to that end, and a courage-fit will very likely replace the fit of fear. Again, in order to feel kindly toward a person to whom we have been inimical, the only way is more or less deliberately to smile, to make sympathetic inquiries, and to force ourselves to say genial things. One hearty laugh together will bring enemies into a closer communion of heart than hours spent on both sides in inward wrestling with the mental demon of uncharitable feeling. To wrestle with a bad feeling only pins our attention on it, and keeps it still fastened in the mind; whereas, if we act as if from some better feeling, the old bad feeling soon folds its tent like an Arab and silently steals away.

From *Talks to Teachers on Psychology* by William James, 1915

71

ON CONQUERING MELANCHOLY BY ACTIVE KINDNESS TO OTHERS

I am tolerably sure you are in the right way; only don't dwell too much upon whatever may have been wrong: to some minds it may be necessary, but not to those who are in danger of becoming indolent by too much thinking about themselves: and when you find yourself, as I dare say you sometimes do, overpowered as it were by melancholy, the best way is to go out, and do something kind to somebody or other. Objects either rich or poor will generally present themselves in the hour of need to those who look for them in earnest, though Oxford is not perhaps the most convenient place to find them in.

However there they surely are if you will take the trouble of looking for them, and perhaps that very trouble is in some sort an advantage in doing away a moody fit … Writing, too, I have known in many cases, a very great relief, but I almost doubt the expediency of preserving journals, at least of looking much back upon them; if one could summon resolution to do so, I fancy the best way would be to write on till one was a little unburthened, and then put one's confessions in the fire. But in all these things, of course no one can judge for his neighbour …

From a letter by John Keble, nineteenth century

72

FOOTPRINTS

One night a man had a dream. He dreamed that he was walking along the beach with the Lord. Across the sky flashed scenes from his life. For each scene he noticed two sets of footprints in the sand; one belonging to himself, and the other to the Lord.

When the last scene of his life flashed before him, he looked back at the footprints in the sand. He noticed that many times during the path of his life there was only one set of footprints. He also noticed that this happened at the very lowest and saddest times of his life.

This really bothered him and he questioned the Lord about it. 'Lord, you said that once I decided to follow you, you'd walk with me all the way. But I have noticed that during the most difficult times in my life, there is only one set of footprints. I don't understand why, when I needed you most, you would leave me?'

Our Lord replied; 'My precious, precious child, I love you and I would never leave you. During your times of trial and suffering, when you see only one set of footprints, it was then that I carried you.'

Author unknown

73

DAYLIGHT

In the name of God, the Compassionate, the Merciful

By the light of day, and by the dark of night, your Lord
has not forsaken you, nor does He abhor you.
The life to come holds a richer prize for you than this
present life. You shall be gratified with what your Lord
will give you.
Did He not find you an orphan and give you shelter?
Did He not find you in error and guide you?

Did He not find you poor and enrich you?
Therefore do not wrong the orphan, nor chide away the beggar. But proclaim the goodness of your Lord.

'Daylight', The Koran 93, 1–11

74

THE LORD IS MY SHEPHERD

The LORD is my shepherd;
I shall not want.
He maketh me to lie down in green pastures: he leadeth me beside the still waters.
He restoreth my soul: he leadeth me in the paths of righteousness for his name's sake.
Yea, though I walk through the valley of the shadow of death, I will fear no evil: for thou art with me; thy rod and thy staff they comfort me.
Thou preparest a table before me in the presence of mine enemies: thou anointest my head with oil; my cup runneth over.
Surely goodness and mercy shall follow me all the days of my life: and I will dwell in the house of the LORD for ever.

Psalm 23:1–6

75

THERE IS MEANING IN UNHAPPINESS

God has created me to do Him some definite service. He has committed some work to me which He has not committed to another. I have my mission. I may never know it in this life, but I shall be told it in the next.

I am a link in the chain, a bond of connection between persons. He has not created me for naught. I shall do good. I shall do His work. I shall be an angel of peace, a preacher of truth in my own place while not intending it – if I do but keep His commandments.

Therefore I will trust Him. Whatever, wherever I am. I can never be thrown away. If I am in sickness, my sickness may serve Him; in perplexity, my perplexity may serve Him; if I am in sorrow, my sorrow may serve Him. He does nothing in vain. He knows what He is about. He may take away my friends, He may throw me among strangers. He may make me feel desolate, make my spirits sink, hide my future from me – still He knows what He is about.

John Henry Newman, nineteenth century

76

DESPAIR AND RECOVERY FROM DESPAIR

It had come to this, that I, a healthy, fortunate man, felt I could no longer live; some irresistible power impelled me to rid myself one way or other of life. I cannot say I *wished* to kill myself. The power which drew me away from life was stronger, fuller, and more widespread than any mere wish. It was a force similar to the former striving to live, only in a contrary direction. All my strength drew me away from life. The thought of self-destruction now came to me as naturally as thoughts of how to improve my life had come formerly. And it was so seductive that I had to be cunning with myself lest I should carry it out too hastily. I did not wish to hurry, because I wanted to use all efforts to disentangle the matter. 'If I cannot unravel matters, there will always be time.' And it was then that I, a man favoured by fortune, hid a cord from myself lest I should hang myself from the crosspiece of the partition in my room where I undressed alone every evening, and I ceased to go out shooting with a gun lest I should be tempted by so easy a way of ending my life. I did not myself know what I wanted; I feared life, desired to escape from it, yet still hoped something of it.

And all this befell me at a time when all around me I had what is considered complete good fortune. I was not yet fifty;

I had a good wife who loved me and whom I loved, good children, and a large estate which without much effort on my part improved and increased. I was respected by my relations and acquaintances more than at any previous time. I was praised by others and without much self-deception could consider that my name was famous ...

During that time this is what happened to me. During that whole year, when I was asking myself almost every moment whether I should not end matters with an noose or a bullet – all that time, together with the course of thought and observation about which I have spoken, my heart was oppressed with a painful feeling, which I can only describe as a search for God.

I say that that search for God was not reasoning, but a feeling, because that search proceeded not from the course of my thoughts – it was even directly contrary to them – but proceeded from the heart. It was a feeling of fear, orphanage, isolation in a strange land, and a hope of help from someone.

Though I was quite convinced of the impossibility of proving the existence of a Deity (Kant had shown, and I quite understood him, that it could not be proved) I yet sought for God, hoped that I should find Him, and from old habit addressed prayers to that which I sought but had not found ...

'He exists,' said I to myself. And I had only for an instant to admit that, and at once life rose within me, and I felt the possibility and joy of being. But again, from the admission of the existence of a God I went on to seek my relation with Him; and again I imagined *that* God – Our Creator in Three Persons who sent His Son, the Saviour – and again *that* God, detached from the world and from me, melted like a block of ice, melted before my eyes, and again nothing remained, and again the spring of life dried up within me, and I despaired and felt that I had nothing to do but to kill myself. And the worst of all was, that I felt I could not do it.

Not twice or three times, but tens and hundreds of times, I reached those conditions, first of joy and animation, and then of despair and consciousness of the impossibility of living.

I remember that it was in early spring: I was alone in the wood listening to its sounds. I listened and thought ever of the same thing, as I had constantly done during those last three years. I was again seeking God.

'Very well, there is no God,' I said to myself; 'there is no one who is not my imagination but a reality like my whole life. He does not exist, and no miracles can prove His existence, because the miracles would be my imagination, besides being irrational.

'But my *perception* of God, of Him whom I seek,' I asked myself, 'where has that perception come from?' And again at this thought the glad waves of life rose within me. All that was around me came to life and received a meaning. But my joy did not last long. My mind continued its work.

'The conception of God is not God,' said I to myself. 'The conception is what takes place within me. The conception of God is something I can evoke or can refrain from evoking in myself. That is not what I seek. I seek that without which there can be no life.' And again all around me and within me began to die, and again I wished to kill myself.

But then I turned my gaze upon myself, on what went on within me, and I remembered all those cessations of life and reanimations that recurred within me hundreds of times. I remembered that I only lived at those times when I believed in God. As it was before, so it was now; I need only be aware of God to live; I need only forget Him, or disbelieve Him, and I died.

What is this animation and dying? I do not live when I lose belief in the existence of God. I should long ago have killed myself had I not had a dim hope of finding Him. I live, really live, only when I feel Him and seek Him. 'What more do you seek?' exclaimed a voice within me. 'This is He. He is that without which one cannot live. To know God and to live is one and the same thing. God is life.'

'Live seeking God, and then you will not live without God.' And more than ever before, all within me and around me lit up, and the light did not again abandon me.

From A *Confession* and *The Gospel in Brief* by Leo Tolstoy, 1828–1910

77

PAIN, FORGIVENESS AND LETTING GO

This passage by Matthew Fox is about accepting pain, rather than trying to escape from it. It is important because the escape from emotional pain may tempt us into refusal of empathy, compulsive working, addiction to alcohol, drugs, gambling or sex. These hide the pain at the expense of being fully human.

Another sinful attitude that the Via Negativa lays bare is the refusal to let pain be pain, the refusal to admit pain, to allow pain, to listen to pain. Or to mystery, to darkness, to the unknown. Too much armour, too heavy defences, too thick walls prevent the vulnerability which is such an occasion of grace in the Via Negativa. We sin against the Via Negativa by refusing to develop our capacities, in this instance our capacities for endurance, our strength for the journey, our strength to endure the pain. The strength called for in the Via Negativa is not a stoical strength of gritting the teeth nor a macho strength of controlling the situation; it is a vulnerable strength, the strength to absorb, to receive the dark with the light, the pain with the pleasure, a strength to keep on falling. It is a strength born of sensitivity, a refusal to live with insensitivity, with coldness of heart, the god of protection, the idol of invulnerability. To be able to undergo what Gandhi calls the 'mountains of suffering' is to discover a new source and a new level of strength. The strength of emptiness, nothingness, the zero point. This strength shatters our very definitions and projections of what it means to be strong.

About Salvation. Salvation, we learn from the Via Negativa, is not a salvation *from pain* but *through pain*. Both Adrienne Rich and Mechtild of Magdeburgh, along with Jesus Christ, speak eloquently to this truth: the need to love our enemies, embrace our fears, enter the darkest of the dark. The very act of entering darkness to befriend it becomes a profoundly healing event. Why is this so? Why are there so many levels of healing or salvation to our befriending of the dark?

The salvation or healing that the Via Negativa is about presents itself in both a personal and a social manner. Of course, since the personal at its depth is social and the social when it is not idolatrised is deeply personal and caring of the individual, this kind of holistic salvation should not surprise anyone. In fact, it ought to constitute a requisite test of all claims to salvation. A personal salvation by itself is not truly salvific, for people in the deepest recesses of their personhood are social. Since they are in deep communion with others, it is their very relationships that beg for healing. Relationships constitute part of the healing of every person. The depth of the personal anguish for healing that the Via Negativa arouses is well attested to by the psalmist.

The enemy pursues my soul;
he has crushed
my life to the ground;
he has made me dwell in darkness
like the dead, long forgotten.
Therefore my spirit fails;
my heart is numb within me.
(Psalm 143:3, 4)

Like water I am poured out,
disjointed are all my bones.
My heart has become like wax,
it is melted within my breast.
Parched as burn clay is my throat,
my tongue cleaves to my jaws.
(Psalm 22:14–16)

By the very acknowledgement of our darkness and of our pain we are saved, that is, healed. By refusing to cover up the cosmic despair and the cosmic anguish that life rains on us we make healing possible. We allow an entrance into the wound to take place. By letting pain be pain we allow healing to be healing, and instead of healing our projections or our imaginary darknesses we heal what is truly in pain, what is deeply and irretrievably dark. Too quickly has the fall/redemption tradition instructed us in the idea that the Via Negativa psalms are 'penitential psalms'. Psalms such as 6, 32, 38, 51, 102, 130, 143 are far bigger than sin and penance meditation. They cover the full range of the Via Negativa experiences of sinking and letting go, of tasting darkness and nothingness, pain and emptying ...

Another reason the Via Negativa fully entered into brings salvation is that such a journey returns us to our origins. Our origins of darkness, of mystery, of deep contentment in the womb. But also to our pre-origins, to our nothingness that preceded our holy and blessed conception. Such an invitation to make the journey full circle is a salvific one for us adults especially, for by making the full connections in our lives we become healed, whole, saved and holy. There is no way to heal without making such full connections.

Forgiveness is another word for letting go. We are saved by forgiveness, the power to forgive ourselves, to allow ourselves to be forgiven, which matures into the power to forgive others and allow them their time to be forgiven. Forgiveness is about letting go of guilt – some imagined, some real – and about letting go of fear. There is no healing, no salvation without forgiveness. And with forgiveness all things become saved and healed once again. Creation is restored.

From *Original Blessing* by Matthew Fox, 1983

78

DESPITE SIN ALL SHALL BE WELL

Another vision of Dame Julian of Norwich. She sees or experiences the vision and reflects on it.

After this the Lord brought to my mind the longing I had to Him before. And I saw that nothing prevented me but sin. And so I looked, generally, upon us all, and thought: *If sin had not been, we should all have been clean and like to our Lord, as He made us.*

And thus in my folly, before this time often I wondered why by the great foreseeing wisdom of God the beginning of sin was not prevented; for then, I thought, all should have been well. This stirring of mind was much to be forsaken, but nevertheless mourning and sorrow I made therefor, without reason and discretion.

But Jesus, who in this vision informed me of all that is needful to me, answered by this word and said: *It behoved that there should be sin; but all shall be well, and all shall be well and all manner of thing shall be well ...*

In this naked word *sin*, our Lord brought to my mind, generally, *all that is not good*, and the shameful despite and the utter setting at nought that He bare for us in this life, and His dying; and all the pains and passions of all His creatures, ghostly and bodily; (for we be all partly set at nought and we shall be set at nought following our Master, Jesus, till we be full purged, that is to say, till we be fully set at nought of our deadly flesh and of all our inward affection which are not very good;) and the beholding of this, with all pains that ever were or ever shall be, – and with all these I understand the passion of Christ for most pain, and overpassing. All this was shown in a touch and quickly passed over into comfort; for our good Lord would not that the soul were frightened of this terrible sight.

But I saw not *sin*: for I believe that it hath no manner of substance nor no part of being, nor could it be known but by the pain it is cause of.

And thus pain, it is something, as to my sight, for a time; for it purges, and makes us to know ourselves and to ask mercy. For the passion of our Lord is comfort to us against all this, and so is His blessed will.

And for the tender love that our good Lord hath to all that shall be saved, He comforts readily and sweetly, signifying thus: *It is truth that sin is the cause of all this pain; but all shall be well, and all shall be well, and all manner of thing shall be well.*

One time our good Lord said: *All thing shall be well*; and another time he said: *Thou shalt see thyself that all MANNER of thing shall be well*; and in these two sayings the soul took sundry understandings.

One was that He wills we know that not only He takes heed to noble things and to great, but also to little and to small, to low and to simple, to one and to other. And so means He in that He says: *ALL MANNER OF THINGS shall be well.* For he wills we know that the least thing shall not be forgotten.

Another understanding is this, that there be deeds evil done in our sight and so great harms taken, that it seems to us that it were impossible that ever it should come to good end. And upon this we look, sorrowing and mourning therefor, so that we cannot resign us unto the blissful beholding of God as we should do. And the cause of this is that the use of our reason is now so blind, so low, and so simple that we cannot know that high marvellous wisdom, the might and the goodness of the blissful Trinity. And thus signifies He when He says: *THOU SHALT SEE THYSELF that all manner of thing shall be well.* As if He said: *Take now heed faithfully and trustingly, and at the last thou shalt verily see it in fulness of joy.*

From *Revelations of Divine Love* by Julian of Norwich, fourteenth century

79

SIN, SEPARATION AND GRACE

Have the men of our time still a feeling of the meaning of sin? Do they, and do we, still realise that sin does *not* mean an immoral act, that 'sin' should never be used in the plural, and that not our sins, but rather our *sin* is the great, all-pervading problem of our life? Do we still know that it is arrogant and erroneous to divide men by calling some 'sinners' and others 'righteous'? For by way of such a division, we can usually discover that we ourselves do not *quite* belong to the 'sinners' since we have avoided heavy sins, have made some progress in control of this or that sin, and have been even humble enough not to call ourselves 'righteous'. Are we still able to realise that this kind of thinking and feeling about sin is far removed from what the great religious tradition, both within and outside the Bible, has meant when it speaks of sin?

I should like to suggest another word to you, not as a substitute for the word 'sin', but as a useful clue in the interpretation of the word 'sin': 'separation'. Separation is an aspect of the experience of everyone. Perhaps the word 'sin' has the same root as the word 'asunder'. In any case, *sin is separation*. To be in a state of sin is to be in the state of separation. And separation is threefold: there is separation among individual lives, separation of a man from himself, and separation of all men from the Ground of Being. This threefold separation constitutes the state of everything that exists; it is a universal fact; it is the fate of every life. And it is our human fate in a very special sense. For *we* as men know that we are separated. We not only suffer with all other creatures because of the self-destructive consequences of our separation, but also know *why* we suffer. We know that we are estranged from something to which we really belong, and with which we *should* be united. We know that the fate of separation is not merely a natural event like a flash of sudden lightning, but that it is an experience in which we actively participate, in which our whole personality is involved, and that, as fate, is it also *guilt*.

Separation which is fate *and* guilt constitutes the meaning of the word 'sin'. It is *this* which is the very state of our entire existence, from its very beginning to its very end. Such separation is prepared in the mother's womb, and before that time, in every preceding generation. It is manifest in the special actions of our conscious life. It reaches beyond our graves into all the succeeding generations. It is our existence itself. *Existence is separation.* Before sin is an act, it is a state ...

Do we know what it means to be struck by grace? It does *not* mean that we suddenly believe that God exists, or that Jesus is the Saviour, or that the Bible contains the truth. To believe that something *is*, is almost contrary to the meaning of grace. Furthermore, grace does not mean simply that we are making progress in our moral self-control, in our fight against special faults, and in our relationships to men and to society. Moral progress may be a fruit of grace, but it is not grace itself, and it can even prevent us from receiving grace. For there is too often a graceless acceptance of Christian doctrines and a graceless battle against the structures of evil in our personalities. Such a graceless relation to God may lead us by necessity either to arrogance or to despair. It would be better to refuse God and the Christ and the Bible than to accept Them without grace. For if we accept without grace, we do so in the state of separation, and can only succeed in deepening the separation. We cannot transform our lives, unless we allow them to be transformed by that stroke of grace. It happens; or it does not happen. And certainly it does *not* happen if we try to force it upon ourselves, just as it shall not happen so long as we think, in our self-complacency, that we have no need of it. Grace strikes us when we are in great pain and restlessness. It strikes us when we walk through the dark valley of a meaningless and empty life. It strikes us when we feel that our separation is deeper than usual, because we have violated another life, a life which we loved, or from which we were estranged. It strikes us when our disgust for our own being, our indifference, our weakness, our hostility, and our lack of direction and composure have become intolerable to us. It strikes us when, year after year, the longed-for perfection of life does not appear, when the old compulsions reign within us as they have for decades, when despair destroys all joy and courage. Sometimes at that moment a wave of light breaks into our darkness, and it is as though a voice were saying: 'You are accepted. *You are accepted*, accepted by that which is greater than you, and the name of which you do not know. Do not ask for the name now; perhaps you will find it later. Do not try to do anything now; perhaps later you will do much. Do not seek for anything; do not perform anything; do not intend anything. *Simply accept the fact that you are accepted!*' If that happens to us, we experience grace. After such an experience we may not be better than before, and we may not believe more than before. But everything is transformed. In that moment, grace conquers sin, and reconciliation bridges the gulf of estrangement. And nothing is demanded of this experience, no religious or moral or intellectual presupposition, nothing but *acceptance*.

From *The Shaking of the Foundations* by Paul Tillich, 1957

CHAPTER SIX

PRAYING AND PRAYERS

I AM VERY BAD AT PRAYING. *I DON'T find it easy and most of the time I don't find it pleasurable. I just find it hard work and not very rewarding. Some of the prayers in this section are here because I think they give insight into the spiritual life, particularly the prayers from different religious traditions. Some, like the surrender prayer, I need almost every day of my life.*

80

PRAYER IS LIKE A LARK SOARING UPWARDS

Prayer is the peace of our spirit, the stillness of our thoughts, the evenness of recollection; the seat of meditation, the rest of our cares, and the calm of our tempest; prayer is the issue of a quiet mind, of untroubled thoughts, it is the daughter of charity, and the sister of meekness; and he that prays to God with an angry, that is, with a troubled and discomposed spirit, is like him that retires into a battle to meditate, and sets up his closet in the out-quarters of an army, and chooses a frontier garrison to be wise in. Anger is a perfect alienation of the mind from prayer, and therefore is contrary to that attention which presents our prayers in a right line to God. For so have I seen a lark rising from his bed of grass and soaring upwards, singing as he rises, and hopes to get to heaven, and climb above the clouds; but the poor bird was beaten back with the loud sighings of an eastern wind, and his motion made irregular and unconstant, descending more at every breath of the tempest, than it could recover by the libration and frequent weighing of its wings; till the little creature was forced to sit down and pant, and stay till the storm was over; and then it made a prosperous flight, and did rise and sing, as if it had learned music and motion from an angel as he passed sometimes through the air about his ministries here below: so is the prayer of a good man; when his affairs have required business, and his business was matter of discipline, and his discipline was to pass upon a sinning person, or had a design of charity, his duty met with infirmities of a man, and anger was its instrument, and the instrument became stronger than the prime agent, and raised a tempest, and overruled the man; and then his prayer was broken, and his thoughts were troubled, and his words went up towards a cloud, and his thoughts pulled them back again, and made them without intention; and the good man sighs for his infirmity, but must be content to lose the prayer, and he must recover it when his anger is removed, and his spirit is becalmed, made even as the brow of Jesus, and smooth like the heart of God; and then it ascends to heaven upon the wings of the holy Dove, and dwells with God, till it returns, like the useful bee, loaden with a blessing and the dew of heaven.

From *The Return of Prayers* by Jeremy Taylor, seventeenth century

81

A NON-RELIGIOUS UNDERSTANDING OF PRAYER

I suspect we have got to ask very seriously whether we should even begin our thinking about prayer in terms of the times we 'set aside', whether prayer is primarily something we do in the 'spaces', in the moments of disengagement from the world. I wonder whether Christian prayer, prayer in the light of the Incarnation, is not to be *defined* in terms of penetration through the world to God rather than of withdrawal from the world to God. For the moment of revelation is precisely so often, in my experience, the moment of meeting and unconditional *engagement*. How easily one finds oneself giving pious advice to a person faced with a decision to 'go away and pray about it'. But, if I am honest, what enlightenment I have had on decisions has almost always come not when I have gone away and stood back from them, but precisely as I have *wrestled through* all the most practical pros and cons, usually with other people. And this activity, undertaken by a Christian trusting and expecting that God is there, would seem to *be* prayer …

Perhaps this is the starting point for a 'non-religious' understanding of prayer. We may begin from the fact that people do give themselves to people. There is nothing 'religious' about this. But to open oneself to another *unconditionally* in love is to be with him in the presence of God, and that is the heart of intercession. To pray for another is to expose both oneself and him to the common ground of our being; it is to see one's concern for him in terms of *ultimate* concern, to let *God* into the relationship. Intercession is to *be with* another at that depth, whether in silence or compassion or action. It may consist simply in listening, when we take the otherness of the other person most seriously. It may not be talking *to* God, as though to a third person, about him at all. The *Thou* addressed may be his own *Thou*, but it may be addressed and responded to at such a level that we can only speak of knowing him in God and God in him. It may not be specifically religious, it may not be consciously Christian: but it may be a meeting of Christ in that man, because his humanity is accepted 'without any reservation'. The way through to the vision of the Son of man and the knowledge of God, which is the heart of contemplative prayer, is by unconditional love of the neighbour of 'the nearest *Thou* to hand'.

Prayer is the responsibility to meet others with *all* I have, to be ready to encounter the unconditional in the conditional, to expect to meet God in the way, not to turn aside from the way. All else is exercise towards that or reflection in depth upon it. It was on the Damascus road that Saul had his encounter with Christ; he was driven to Arabia by it. He did not have to go to Arabia to seek God; but equally from Arabia he returned deepened in the power of the Spirit. There is an inescapable dialectic of engagement and withdrawal. But much depends on which we regard as primary. There is no sense in which a Christian *has* to turn aside from the world in order to meet God – any more than the holy of holies is for him in the sanctuary. But there is a sense in which he *has* to go into the world, in unconditional love, in order to meet God; for 'God is love' and 'he who does not love does not know God'.

From *Honest to God* by John Robinson, 1963

82

THE PRACTICE OF THE PRESENCE OF GOD

The first time I saw Brother Lawrence was upon the 3rd of August, 1666. He told me that God had done him a singular favour in his conversation at the age of eighteen…

He told me that all consists in one hearty renunciation of everything which we are sensible does not lead to God; that we might accustom ourselves to a continued conversation with Him with freedom and in simplicity …

That when an occasion of practising some virtue offered he addressed himself to God, saying, 'Lord, I cannot do this unless Thou enablest me' and that then he received strength more than sufficient.

That when he had failed in his duty, he only confessed his

fault, saying to God, 'I shall never do otherwise if You leave me to myself; 'tis You must hinder my falling and mend what is amiss.' That after this he gave himself no further uneasiness about it …

That our sanctification did not depend upon changing our works, but in doing that for God's sake which we commonly do for our own. That it was lamentable to see how many people mistook the means for the end, addicting themselves to certain works which they performed very imperfectly by reason of their human or selfish regards.

That the most excellent method he had found of going to God was that of doing our common business without any view of pleasing men, and (as far as we are capable) purely for the love of God …

That we ought not to be weary of doing little things for the love of God, Who regards not the greatness of the work, but the love with which it is performed. That we should not wonder if in the beginning we often failed in our endeavours, but that at last we should gain a habit which will naturally produce its acts in us without our care and to our exceeding great delight …

That in the beginning of his noviciate [at the monastery] he spent the hours appointed for private prayer in thinking of God, so as to convince his mind of, and to impress deeply upon his heart, the divine existence rather by devout sentiments and submission to the lights of faith than by studied reasonings and elaborate meditations. That by this short and sure method he exercised himself in the knowledge and love of God, resolving to use his utmost endeavour to live in a continual sense of His presence, and, if possible, never to forget Him more.

That when he had thus in prayer filled his mind with great sentiments of that infinite being he went to his work appointed in the kitchen (for he was cook to the society); there, having first considered severally the things his office required done, he spent all the intervals of his time, as well before as after his work, in prayer.

That when he began his business he said to God, with a filial trust in Him, 'O my God since Thou art with me, and I must now in obedience to Thy commands, apply my mind to these outward things, I beseech Thee to grant me the grace to continue in Thy presence; and to this end do Thou prosper me with Thy assistance, receive all my works, and possess all my affections.'

As he proceeded in his work he continued his familiar conversation with his Maker, imploring His grace and offering to Him all his actions.

When he had finished he examined himself how he had discharged his duty; if he found *well*, he returned thanks to God; if otherwise, he asked pardon; and without being discouraged he set his mind right again, and continued his exercise of the *presence of God* as if he had never deviated from it. 'Thus,' said he,' by rising after my falls, and by frequently renewed acts of faith and love, I am come to a state wherein it would be as difficult for me not to think of God as it was at first to accustom myself to it.'

As Brother Lawrence had found such an advantage in walking in the presence of God, it was natural for him to recommend it earnestly to others; but his example was a stronger inducement than any arguments he could propose. His very countenance was edifying; such a sweet and calm devotion appearing in it as could not but affect the beholders. And it was observed that in the greatest hurry of business in the kitchen he still preserved his recollection and heavenly-mindedness. He was never hasty or loitering, but did each thing in its season, with an even uninterrupted composure and tranquillity of spirit. 'The time of business,' said he, 'does not with me differ from the time of prayer; and in the noise and clutter of my kitchen, while several persons are at the same time calling for different things, I possess God in as great tranquillity as if I were upon my knees at the Blessed Sacrament.'

From *The Practice of the Presence of God* by Brother Lawrence, 1692

83

THE PARADOX OF PRAYER

I asked for strength that I might achieve;
I was made weak that I might learn humbly to obey.
I asked for health that I might do greater things;
I was given infirmity that I might do better things.
I asked for riches that I might be happy;
I was given poverty that I might be wise.
I asked for power that I might have the praise of men;
I was given weakness that I might feel the need of God.
I asked for all things that I might enjoy life;
I was given life that I might enjoy all things.
I got nothing that I had asked for,
But everything I had hoped for.
Almost despite myself my unspoken prayers were answered;
I am, among all men, most richly blessed.

Prayer of an unknown Confederate soldier

84

OUR FATHER

Our Father, which art in heaven,
Hallowed be thy name.
Thy kingdom come.
Thy will be done in earth, as it is in heaven.
Give us this day our daily bread.
And forgive us our trespasses, as we forgive them that trespass against us.
And lead us not into temptation;
But deliver us from evil:
Amen.

From *The Book of Common Prayer*, 1662

85

THE PRAYER OF THE SABBATH LIGHTS

Lord of the Universe, I am about to perform the *mitzvah* [sacred duty] of kindling the lights in honour of the Sabbath, as it is written: 'And thou shall call the Sabbath a delight, and the holy day of the Lord a day to be honoured.' In merit of this *mitzvah*, bestow upon me and my family a full life. Be gracious to us and bless us with abundant blessings, and cause Your Presence to dwell among us.

Father of Mercy, continue Your lovingkindness unto me and to my dear ones. Make me worthy [to rear my children so that they] walk before You in the way of the righteous, loyal to Your Torah [law], and clinging to good deeds. Keep away from us all manner of shame, grief and sorrow. Grant that peace, light and joy, always remain on our home. For with You is the fountain of life; in Your light do we see light. Amen.

From *The Jewish Authorised Daily Prayer Book*, current edition

86

ETERNAL LIGHT, SHINE INTO OUR HEARTS

Eternal Light, shine into our hearts;
Eternal Goodness, deliver us from evil;
Eternal Power, be our support;
Eternal Wisdom, scatter the darkness of our ignorance;
Eternal Pity, have mercy upon us;
That with all our hearts and mind and soul and strength we may seek thy face and be brought by thine infinite mercy to thy holy presence, through Jesus Christ our Lord.

Prayer of Alcuin, eighth century

87

LORD, MAKE ME A CHANNEL OF THY PEACE

Lord, make me a channel of your peace,
That where there is hatred I may bring love;
That where there is wrong, I may bring the spirit of forgiveness;
That where there is discord, I may bring harmony;
That where there is error I may bring truth;
That where there is doubt I may bring faith;
That where there is despair I may bring hope;
That where there are shadows I may bring your light;
And where there is sadness, I may bring joy.
Lord, grant that I may seek rather to comfort than to be comforted,
To understand than to be understood,
To love than to be loved:
For it is by giving that one receives,
It is by self-forgetting that one finds,
It is by forgiving that one is forgiven,
It is by dying that one awakens to eternal life.

Prayer of St Francis of Assisi, twelfth century

88

ST PATRICK'S BREASTPLATE

I bind myself today to the virtue of Heaven,
In light of sun,
In brightness of snow,
In splendour of fire,
In speed of lightning,
In swiftness of wind,
In depth of sea,
In stability of earth,
In compactness of rock.
I bind myself today to God's virtue to pilot me,
God's might to uphold me,
God's wisdom to guide me,
God's eye to look before me,
God's ear to hear me,
God's word to speak for me,
God's hand to guard me,
God's way to lie before me,
God's shield to protect me …
Christ with me, Christ before me, Christ behind me, Christ in me!
Christ below me, Christ above me, Christ at my right hand, Christ at my left.

Christ in breadth, Christ in length, Christ in height!
Christ in the mouth of every one who speaks to me,
Christ in every eye who sees me,
Christ in every ear who hears me …

Prayer attributed St Patrick, fourth century

89

SOCRATES' PRAYER

Beloved Pan, and all other gods who here abide, grant us to be beautiful in the inner man, and all that we have of outer things to be at peace with those within. Counting only the wise to be truly rich, increase to all here their store of gold.

From *The Phaedo* by Plato, fourth century BC

90
SLOW ME DOWN, LORD!

Slow me down, Lord! Ease the pounding of my heart by the quietening of my mind. Steady my hurried pace with a vision of the eternal reach of time. Give me, amid the confusion of the day, the calmness of the everlasting hills. Break the tensions of my nerves and muscles with the soothing music of the singing streams. Help me to know the magical, restoring power of sleep.

Teach me the art of taking minute vacations ... of slowing down to look at a flower, to chat with a friend, to pat a dog, to read a few lines from a good book. Remind me each day of the fable of the hare and the tortoise, that I may know that the race is not always to the swift; that there is more to life than increasing its speed.

Let me look upwards into the branches of the towering oak and know that it grew great and strong because it grew slowly and well. Slow me down, Lord, and inspire me to send my roots deep into the soil of life's enduring values that I may grow towards the stars of my greater destiny.

Orin L. Crain, date unknown

91

THE PRAYER OF THE TAILOR

O God, I am Mustafah, the tailor, and I work at the shop of Muhammad Ali. The whole day long I sit and pull the needle and the thread through the cloth. O God, you are the needle and I am the thread. I am attached to you and I follow you. When the thread tries to slip away from the needle it becomes tangled up and must be cut so that it can be put back in the right place. O God, help me to follow you wherever you may lead me. For I am really only Mustafah, the tailor, and I work at the shop of Muhammad Ali on the great square.

Author unknown

92

PRAYER OF SURRENDER

Dear God,

Today, I acknowledge, accept and admit that my life is a God-job, and I surrender my life to you.

Today, I surrender fear, doubt, worry, anxiety and control.

Today, I acknowledge, accept and admit that I cannot fix anyone or anything.

Today, I acknowledge, accept and admit that I cannot change anyone or anything.

Today, I acknowledge, accept and admit that I cannot heal anyone or anything.

Today, I acknowledge, accept and admit that I cannot help anyone.

Today, I acknowledge, accept and admit that I cannot control anyone or anything.

Today, I acknowledge, accept and admit that I cannot fix, change, heal or help myself.

I am a God-job. My life is a God-job.

Today, dear God, please work on me, in me, through me. Work on my life, my relationships, all of my affairs, on everyone and everything in my life.

Today, dear God, please have your perfect way with me, for I know that the least you can be to me and for me is good.

For this I am so grateful.
And So It Is!

From *Every Day I Pray* by Iyanla Vanzant, 2001

93

FURNISH THE EVENING WITH BRIGHTNESS

The day is over, and I give you thanks, O Lord.
Evening is at hand; furnish it with brightness.
Each day has its evening, and so also has life.
The evening of life is age.
Age has overtaken me; furnish it with brightness.
Do not forsake me now that my strength is failing;
But bear me, carry me, deliver me, to my old age,
To the time of my white hair.
Stay with me, Lord, for evening is coming,
And the day of this fretful life is far spent,
May your strength be made perfect in my weakness.

'An Evening Prayer', by Lancelot Andrewes, sixteenth century

94
PRAYERS FOR FELLOW PRISONERS

This prayer was written by Dietrich Bonhoeffer, as he awaited execution in a Nazi concentration camp.

Christmas 1943

Morning Prayers

O God, early in the morning I cry to you.
Help me to pray
And to concentrate my thoughts on you;
I cannot do this alone.

In me there is darkness,
But with you there is light;
I am lonely, but you do not leave me;
I am feeble in heart, but with you there is help;
I am restless, but with you there is peace.
In me there is bitterness, but with you there is patience;
I do not understand your ways,
But you know the way for me.

O heavenly Father,
I praise and thank you
For the peace of the night:
I praise and thank you for this new day;
I praise and thank you for all your goodness
and faithfulness throughout my life.

You have granted me many blessings;
Now let me also accept what is hard
from your hand.
You will lay on me no more
than I can bear.
You make all things work together for good
for your children.

Lord Jesus Christ,
You were poor
and in distress, a captive and forsaken as I am.
You know all man's troubles;
You abide with me
when all men fail me;
You remember and seek me;
It is your will that I should know you
and turn to you.
Lord, I hear your call and follow;
Help me.

O Holy Spirit,
Give me faith that will protect me
from despair, from passions, and from vice;
Give me such love for God and men
as will blot out all hatred and bitterness;
Give me the hope that will deliver me
From fear and faint-heartedness.

O holy and merciful God,
my Creator and Redeemer,
my Judge and Saviour,
You know me and all that I do.
You hate and punish evil without respect of persons
in this world and the next;
You forgive the sins of those
who sincerely pray for forgiveness;
You love goodness, and reward it on this earth
with a clear conscience,
and, in the world to come,
with a crown of righteousness.

I remember in your presence all my loved ones,
my fellow prisoners, and all who in this house
perform their hard service;
Lord, have mercy.
Restore me to liberty,
and enable me so to live now
that I may answer before you and before men.
Lord, whatever this day may bring,
Your name be praised.
Amen.

From *Prisoner of God: Letters and Papers from Prison*, by Dietrich Bonhoeffer, 1951

CHAPTER SEVEN

MORTALITY AND DEATH

ACCEPTING MY OWN MORTALITY, *the certainty of my own death, is important to me. If I can accept that each hour brings my death closer, then my life is more precious to me. These passages give me inspiration for this. Dying is part of my spiritual journey, and I hope that I shall have the courage to meet my death, when it comes, with a ready acceptance, though I fear it greatly.*

95

TO EVERYTHING THERE IS A TIME ...

To every thing there is a season, and a time to every purpose under the heaven:

A time to be born, and a time to die; a time to plant, and a time to pluck up that which is planted;

A time to kill, and a time to heal; a time to break down, and a time to build up;

A time to weep, and a time to laugh; a time to mourn, and a time to dance;

A time to cast away stones, and a time to gather stones together; a time to embrace, and a time to refrain from embracing;

A time to get, and a time to lose; a time to keep, and a time to cast away;

A time to rend, and a time to sew; a time to keep silence, and a time to speak;

A time to love, and a time to hate; a time of war, and a time of peace.

What profit hath he that worketh in that wherein he laboureth?

I have seen the travail, which God hath given to the sons of men to be exercised in it.

He hath made every thing beautiful in his time: also he hath

set the world in their heart, so that no man can find out
the work that God maketh from the beginning to the end.
I know that there is no good in them, but for a man to
rejoice, and to do good in his life.
And also that every man should eat and drink, and enjoy the
good of all his labour, it is the gift of God.
I know that, whatsoever God doeth, it shall be for ever:
nothing can be put to it, nor any thing taken from it: and
God doeth it, that men should fear before him.
That which hath been is now; and that which is to be hath
already been; and God requireth that which is past.

Ecclesiastes 3:1–15

96

THE SPARROW IN THE HALL

King Eadwine of Northumbria, who was considering converting to Christianity, consulted first with his aldermen and counsellors. One of his aldermen had this to say about the shortness and uncertainty of our life on earth.

Such appears to me, O King, this present life of men on earth in comparison of the time that is unknown to us, – so like as if you were sitting at a banquet with your aldermen and thanes, in wintertime, and a fire was kindled, and your palace warmed, and it rained and snowed, and stormed outside; then came a sparrow and quickly flew through the hall; and came in through one door, and went out through another. Lo! In the time that he is within, he is not touched by the storm of the winter; but that is only an eye-blink, and the least space; and soon he goes from winter to winter again. So this life of men appears for a short space: what goes before it, or what follows after it, we know not. Therefore if this new lore brings anything more certain and more suitable, it is worthy of this, that we follow it.

From *Ecclesiastical History of the English People* by Bede, eighth century

97

THE DEATH OF SOCRATES

Socrates, the philosopher, was charged with corrupting the youth of Athens, and condemned to death by poison. His last day was spent with his friends in prison discussing the immortality of the soul. Then the gaoler told him it was time to take the hemlock, which would kill him.

Socrates looked up at him, and replied, 'Farewell: I will do as you say.' Then he turned to us and said, 'How courteous the man is! And the whole time that I have been here, he has constantly come in to see me, and sometimes he has talked to me, and has been the best of men; and now, how generously he weeps for me! Come, Crito, let us obey him: let the poison be brought if it is ready; and if it is not ready, let it be prepared.'

Crito replied: 'Nay, Socrates, I think that the sun is still upon the hills; it has not set. Besides, I know that other men take the poison quite late, and eat and drink heartily, and even enjoy the company of their chosen friends, after the announcement has been made. So do not hurry; there is still time.'

Socrates replied, 'And those whom you speak of, Crito, naturally do so; for they think that they will be gainers by so doing. And I naturally shall not do so; for I think that I should gain nothing by drinking the poison a little later, but my own contempt for so greedily saving up a life which is already spent. So do not refuse to do as I say.'

Then Crito made a sign to his slave who was standing by; and the slave went out, and after some delay returned with the man who was to give the poison, carrying it prepared in a cup. When Socrates saw him, he asked, 'You understand these things, my good sir, what have I to do?'

'You have only to drink this,' he replied, 'and to walk about until your legs feel heavy, and then lie down; and it will act of itself.' With that he handed the cup to Socrates, who took it quite cheerfully without trembling and without any change of colour or of feature, and looked up at the man with that fixed glance of his, and asked, 'What say you to making a libation (*pouring out a little as an offering to the gods*) from this draught? May I, or not?'

'We only prepare so much as we think sufficient, Socrates,' he answered. 'I understand,' said Socrates. 'But I suppose that I may, and must, pray to the gods that my journey hence may be prosperous: that is my prayer; be it so.' With these words he put the cup to his lips and drank the poison quite calmly and cheerfully.

Till then most of us had been able to control our grief fairly well; but when we saw him drinking, and then the poison finished, we could do so no longer: my tears came fast in spite of myself, and I covered my face and wept for myself: it was not for him, but at my own misfortune in losing such a friend. Even before that Crito had been unable to restrain his tears, and had gone away; and Apollodorus, who had never once ceased weeping the whole time, burst into a loud cry, and made us one and all break down by his sobbing and grief, except only Socrates himself.

'What are you doing, my friends?' he exclaimed. 'I sent away the women chiefly in order that they might not offend in this way; for I have heard that a man should die in silence. So calm yourself and bear up.'

When we heard that, we were ashamed and we ceased from weeping. But he walked about, until he said that his legs were getting heavy, and then he lay down on his back, as he was told. And the man who gave the poison began to examine his feet and legs from time to time: then he pressed his foot hard, and asked if there was any feeling in it; and Socrates said, 'No' and then his legs, and so higher and higher, and showed us that he was cold and stiff.

And Socrates felt himself, and said that when it came to his heart, he should be gone. He was already growing cold about the groin, when he uncovered his face, which had been covered, and spoke for the last time. 'Crito,' he said, 'I owe a cock to Asclepius (*the offering made to the god on recovering from an illness*); do not forget to pay it.'

'It shall be done,' replied Crito. 'Is there anything else that you wish?' He made no answer to this question; but after a short interval there was a movement, and the man uncovered him, and his eyes were fixed. Then Crito closed his mouth and his eyes.

Such was the end of our friend, a man, I think, who was the wisest and justest, and the best man I have ever known.

From *The Phaedo* by Plato, fourth century BC

98

FOR WHOM THE BELL TOLLS

Perchance he for whom this bell tolls may be so ill as that he knows not it tolls for him, and perchance I may think myself so much better than I am as that they who are about me and see my state may have caused it to toll for me and I know not that.

The Church is catholic, universal; so are all her actions. All that she does belongs to all. When she baptises a child, that action concerns me, for that child is thereby connected to that head which is my head too, and engrafted into that body whereof I am a member. And when she buries a man, that action concerns me: all of mankind is of one author and one volume. When one man dies, one chapter is not torn out of the book but translated into a better language, and every chapter must be so translated. God employs several translators. Some pieces are translated by age, some by sickness, some by war, some by justice. But God's hand is in every translation, and his hand shall bind up all our scattered leaves again for that library where every book shall lie open to one another.

As therefore the bell that rings to sermon calls not upon the preacher only but upon the congregation to come, so this bell calls us all. But how much more me, who am brought so near the door by this sickness? There was a contention, as far as a lawsuit, in which both piety and dignity, religion and estimation, were mingled, which of the religious orders should ring to prayers first in the morning; and it was determined that they should ring first that rose earliest. If we understand aright the dignity of this bell that tolls for our evening prayer, we would be glad to make it ours by rising early, in that application that it should be ours as well as his whose indeed it is. The bell doth toll for him that thinks it doth. And though it intermit again, yet from that minute that that occasion wrought upon him, he is united to God.

Who casts not up his eye to the sun when it rises? But who takes off his eye from the comet when that breaks out? Who bends not his ear to any bell which upon any occasion rings?

But who can remove it from that bell which is passing a piece of himself out of this world? No man is an island entire of itself; every man is a piece of the continent, a part of the main. If a clod be washed away by the sea, Europe is the less, as well as if a promontory were, as well as if a manor of thy friend's or thine own were. Any man's death diminishes me, because I am involved in mankind. And therefore never send to know for whom the bell tolls: it tolls for thee.

No man hath affliction enough that is not matured and ripened by it, and made fit for God by that affliction. If a man carry treasure in bullion, or in wedge of gold, and have none coined into current monies, his treasure will not defray him as he travels. Tribulation is treasure in the nature of it, but is not current money in the use of it except we get nearer and nearer our home, heaven, by it. Another man may be sick too, and sick to death, and this affliction may lie in his bowels as gold in a mine and be of no use to him. But this bell, that tells me of his affliction, digs out and applies that gold to me if, by this consideration of another's danger, I take mine own into contemplation, and so secure myself by making my recourse to my God, who is our only security.

From *The Devotions* by John Donne, 1623

99

THE TRUMPETS ON THE OTHER SIDE

Then Mr Honest called for his friends, and said unto them, 'I die, but shall make no will. As for my honesty, it shall go with me; let him that comes after be told of this.'

When the day he was to be gone, was come, he addressed himself to go over the River. Now the River at that time overflowed the banks in some places. But Mr Honest in his lifetime had spoken to one Good-conscience to meet him there, the which he also did, and lent him his hand, and so helped him over. The last words of Mr Honest were, 'Grace reigns.' So he left the world.

After this, it was noised abroad that Mr Valiant-for-Truth was taken with a summons, by the same Post as the other … When he understood it, he called for his friends, and told them of it. Then said he, 'I am going to my fathers, and though with great difficulty I am got hither, yet now I do not repent me of all the trouble I have been at to arrive where I am. My sword I give to him that shall succeed me in my pilgrimage, and my courage and skill to him that can get it. My marks and scars I carry with me, to be a witness for me that I have fought his battles who now will be my rewarder.'

When the day that he must go hence was come many accompanied him to the River side, into which, as he went, he said, '*Death, where is thy sting?*' And as he went down deeper, he said, '*Grave, where is thy victory?*' So he passed over, and the trumpets sounded for him on the other side.

From *Pilgrim's Progress* by John Bunyan, 1678

100

A PRAYER FOR THE DEAD

Go forth upon thy journey from the world, Christian soul!
Go from this world! Go, in the name of God,
The omnipotent Father, who created thee!
Go, in the name of Jesus Christ, our Lord,
Son of the living God, who bled for thee!
Go, in the name of the Holy Spirit, who
Hath been poured out on thee! Go in the name
Of Angels and Archangels; in the name
Of Thrones and Dominations; in the name
Of Princedoms and of Powers; and in the name
Of Cherubim and Seraphim, go forth!

From *The Dream of Gerontius* by John Henry Newman, 1865

NOTES

CHAPTER ONE – THE HOLINESS OF CREATION AND CREATURES

1. Your Enjoyment of the World …

Thomas Traherne (1636–74) was a priest, poet and mystic, who led an obscure life in an England torn by the Civil War. A great mystic – for me the greatest. I could fill this book with his prose and poetry and think every essay and poem one of the greatest in the world. A collection of his meditations was found in manuscript and published as *Centuries of Meditations* in 1908.

2. The Beginning of Creation

This powerful, Old Testament myth of creation tells us that the natural world is good. All nature, even snakes and reptiles, is good. Some religious people have sometimes despised the world. The creation story makes it clear that God loved the world from the very beginning. And so should we. And if we love it, we should care for it.

3. Light

The Koran – also spelled 'Qur'an' – 'The Recitation', is regarded by Muslims as the infallible Word of God, a transcription of a heavenly message which was revealed to the Prophet Muhammad during his ministry on earth. It is at the centre of Islam. The Qur'an consists of 114 surahs [chapters], arranged according to length, with the longer surahs first. Many verses are extremely beautiful in their original language apparently. I love this passage.

4. God in the World

The founder of Sikhism, Siri Guru Nanak Dev (1469–1539), was a poet and a religious leader who believed that love of God implied love for his creation. Those that love, serve. He spoke in favour of the downtrodden and in favour of women. He believed that in God's eyes there were no religious distinctions and he had no time for sectarianism. He believed that true worship was a matter of the heart, not the rite. I don't know where these poetic lines come from.

5. Seeing the World

Most people only know William Blake (1757–1827) from his poems about the lamb and the tiger, yet he wrote stupendous books of poetic prophecy.

A great poet, he was also a fine artist and a true mystic. William Blake talked with angels and once saw a fairy funeral. He died singing. These paragraphs and sentences of his come from his letter 'To Revd. Dr Trusler', from the end of *The Vision of the Last Judgement* and from *The Marriage of Heaven and Hell*.

6. Cherry Blossom and Transience

This is an essay from *The Tusrezuregusa of Kenko*. Kenko (a.k.a. Yoshida No Kaneyoshi, 1283–1350) was a Japanese Buddhist priest, a courtier and an essayist. The Japanese celebrate the coming of cherry blossom in the spring. It has a spiritual meaning. The coming and going of blossom emphasises the transience of life. Unlike we in the West who prize permanence and what we consider perfection (the flower in full bloom, for instance), they prize transience and imperfection. They understand that true enjoyment of the blossom's beauty depends on its fragility. If we remember this, we see the world with new eyes.

7. Blessings on Various Occasions

These blessings come from the Jewish prayer book. Each blessing makes us prize, rather than despise, the world and its beauties.

8. The Spirituality of the Land to Native Americans

The usually published version of this passage, attributed to Chief Seathl or Seattle, was written by a Hollywood script writer and was only very loosely based on this original. This is the text of his speech to the Commissioner of Indian Affairs for the Washington Territories, which was recorded on 10 January 1854 by Dr Henry Smith and printed in *Seattle Sunday Star* some years later, in 1887. Seathl was a Duwamish, known for his courage and bearing when a young warrior, and leader of six of the local tribes. He was in his late fifties or sixties when he made this speech.

9. Deep Peace of the Running Wave

I first heard this in an open-air service at the site of a lost medieval church. I have no idea where it comes from. Some argue that the concept of a nature-loving Celtic spirituality has no basis in history – but it surely has a message for us today, even.

10. Thanksgivings for the Body

The Thanksgivings are to be found in *A Serious and Pathetical Contemplation of the Mercies of God in several most Devout and Sublime Thanksgivings for the Same*, published anonymously in 1699. It was written by Thomas Traherne (see 1), probably quite early on in his life but published only after his death.

11. Thanking God for the Body's Passages

The Asher Yatzar prayer from the Jewish prayer book, which follows a prayer for washing hands. There is nothing here of the unhealthy Christian tradition of disgust for the body. This is a prayer used when going to the lavatory.

12. St Benno and the Frog

Extracts 12 to 14 come from *Beasts and Saints*, edited and translated by the great medieval Latin translator, Helen Waddell, and originally published in 1934. St Benno (1010–1106) was Bishop of Meissen in Germany and the patron saint of Munich. This story about the frogs comes from his biography, written by Jerome Emser in 1512.

13. St Godric and the Reptiles

St Godric (1065–1170) was a ship's captain turned hermit after a pilgrimage to Jerusalem. He went barefoot because Jesus had. This extract comes from a biography written by his contemporary, Reginald of Durham.

14. St Kevin and the Blackbird

St Kevin (d. 618) was a prince of the royal line in Leinster, in Ireland. He chose a hermit's life in Glendalough, which became a large monastic centre. Many stories are told about his love and care for animals. This translation comes from a collection of Latin manuscripts printed in *Vitae Sanctorum Hiberniae*, 1910. I found it in *Beasts and Saints* (see 12).

15. The Prophet Muhammad and the Baby Birds

The *Hadith* are the traditional and authorised stories attributed to the Prophet Muhammad. Each story is preceded by its provenance, who heard it and told whom. Each is a source of guidance in Islam for the community. The *Hadith* make it clear that the Prophet Muhammad was kind and loving to domestic animals and unusually sensitive to the needs of wild creatures.

16. The Wonder of the Behemoth

This passage occurs when Job has questioned God's justice and goodness. God declares his power and follows this with a description of the behemoth and the leviathan (which I haven't included). God is telling Job of the power, might and awe of his creation. Some commentators thought the behemoth was an elephant but it was more probably a hippopotamus.

17. A Prayer for Animals

St Basil (329–79) was an early bishop who campaigned against the heresy of Arianism. But he had his gentler side. He left behind nine Lenten sermons on the days of creation, in which he says that the beauty of the world reflects the splendour of God. I don't know where, in his body of work, this prayer comes from.

CHAPTER TWO – THE WAY OF THE MYSTIC

18. The Valley of the Dry Bones

This is one of the most mysterious and moving texts of the Old Testament. It is about the power of God to renew the people of Israel, the power to renew us too to a new life. There's another mysterious vision in Ezekiel (not in this book) in which the prophet sees an angelic wheel – worth reading for its strangeness. I find it interesting that the *Tao Te Ching* (see 21) also speaks of the significance of a wheel.

19. Trying to Understand God

The son of a shoemaker, Jacob Bauthumley or Bottomley (1613–85) was an early nonconformist, one of the Ranters (as their enemies called them). He became a quartermaster in the Parliamentary army during the English Civil War but in 1650 was dismissed from the service and punished by having his tongue pierced as a punishment for blasphemy. His book, *The Light and Dark Sides of God*, has been described as 'a neglected masterpiece of seventeenth-century devotional prose'. It deserves to be better known.

20. In the Beginning Was the Word

One of the most beautiful passages of the New Testament. The Gospel of St John is a literary, as well as a spiritual, triumph. It is also the Gospel that takes the story of the Jewish teacher and Messiah and changes it to the story of the son of God and the founder of Christianity. This is one of the spiritual passages that makes the hair stand up on the back of my neck. It describes a God who suffered with us and for us.

21. Tao – The Way and Its Power

The *Tao Te Ching* is one of the most mysterious texts in the world. Every Chinese character has several meanings. I struggled with eight different translations, each more different than the last! Lao Tzu (born c. 604 BC) was the court architect, but he left the court and journeyed west. At the Han-Ku Pass, the keeper of the pass begged him to compose a book. He did so and then disappeared. The meaning of this passage is to me an intuitive one, a meaning which is as much between the words as through them. This book resonates in my mind. The passages are from Chapters 1, 4 and 11.

22. Julian of Norwich is Shown a Little Thing

Dame Julian of Norwich (1342–c.1413) was an anchoress enclosed in a small cell. At the age of thirty, she was severely ill and expected to die. On the fourth day she received the last rites. It was after this that she received her visions. Her account of these was (unusually) written in English not Latin and in 1901 was updated by Grace Warrack. I am using her version, occasionally taking out some (not all) of the archaic words for easier reading. Julian saw the femininity of God and her message seems right for our times.

23. Some Proverbs of Paradox

I have left out some of the more difficult of William Blake's proverbs, because they would need too much explanation and you have to read them not literally but realising that they teach by paradox, shock and exaggeration. 'Without contraries there is no progression,' he wrote. He saw that energy, love, and forgiveness (not just restraint and religious rules) were important to a spiritual life. He knew that comparisons between self and others were damaging.

24. Learning from a Little Child

It's remarkable how little attention Christians pay to this teaching. Famous Christians like St Augustine, with his emphasis on original sin, have ignored it altogether. If we took it seriously we adults would attend Sunday school to be taught by children! Instead we persist in teaching them instead of learning from them. A pity.

25 Pagan Nature Mysticism

Modern paganism, Wicca in particular, is in the tradition of finding the divine in the world, particularly the natural world, rather than outside it. It is the only modern religion I know that sees the divine as equally as much female as male. Wicca suffers from the same 'blood libel' that was used to justify the persecution of the Jews – made-up stories about the evil occult. A bit earlier in this service comes the sentence 'my law is love unto all beings'.

26. Earth Mystery and Mysticism

An essayist, nature writer and novelist, Richard Jefferies (1848–87) is now sadly undervalued. His mysticism is not dependent on a belief in God or in any kind of theology. He experienced the divine in nature. Here is a spiritual experience open to the atheist, not just the believer. *The Story of My Heart* is a neglected spiritual masterpiece.

CHAPTER THREE – HOW TO LIVE AND WORK

27. Look to This Day

I just don't know where this comes from but I very much like the message. Learning to live in the day is a powerful tool for living without regret and anger (from the past) or fear and apprehension (about the future).

28. The Ten Commandments

You could call this the original quick guide to religious and community life! These commandments belong to both Judaism and Christianity and have formed the moral landscape of the West. The social rules are almost all negative and most of us confidently ignore the prohibition against graven images.

29. Jesus Gives the Sermon on the Mount

This is teaching that asks us to go beyond the Ten Commandments – a powerful plea not just for the actions of forgiveness and love, but for their presence in the heart. This is as St Francis said: 'Live the word. If you must, speak it.'

30. Arjuna the Warrior Asks the God Krishna How to Live

The 'Bhagavad-Gita', part of India's great epic poem, the *Mahabharata*, was probably written somewhere between 500 and 200 BC. Krishna explains how a man should act in this world. Right action is chosen by renouncing the fruits or rewards of action, by concentrating on what is one's duty and leaving the outcome to God.

31. Starting Each Day the Stoic Way

Acceptance is the key quality in the *Meditations* of the Roman emperor and stoic, Marcus Aurelius (121–80). As a young man he was influenced by Stoic philosophy and by the writings of Epictetus. The Stoics maintained that what was important was the state of a man's soul – his conscience and integrity – not outward circumstances such as life and death, reputation, pleasures or pains, or riches or poverty. However irritating or even evil men are, we should preserve that integrity and not return evil for evil. Ironically Marcus Aurelius persecuted Christians during his reign.

32. How Thinking Leads to Happiness or Unhappiness

The *Dhammapada*, translated either 'Words of the Doctrine' or 'Way of Truth', is a Buddhist book of aphorisms, said to be spoken by the Buddha himself. One of the great spiritual masterpieces of the world, the original text is witty as well as wise. It is part of a collection of texts, the *Khuddaka Nikaya*, which is one of five collections found in the *Sutta Pitaka*, a very early body of texts written between 500 BC and the Christian era.

33. The Tao and the Actionless Way

This is the paradoxical message of Taoism – that less may mean more. If we look at life in the right way, we will stay serene. Taoism is about going with the flow of things rather than fighting against fate, participation rather than intervention and control. In this last, it is in opposition to the Western emphasis on action at all costs. The Tao reminds us that intelligence is not necessarily helpful in the things that really matter. The *Tao Te Ching* fascinates me. These passages are from Chapters 16, 44 and 47.

34. The Jewish Fathers' Thoughts on Living

These sayings are found in Chapters 1, 2, 3 and 4 of 'Ethics of the Fathers', a collection of sayings by notable Jewish teachers. Hillel Hababli, who was active 30 BC to 10 AD, was a rabbi said to be the embodiment of humility and kindness. He also said: 'Whatever is hateful to you, do not do to others; this is the whole Torah, the rest is commentary.' Rabbi Elazar ben Azariah (70–135 AD) held high office. Simeon ben Zoma was a great scholar who died young. His four questions here are famous gnomic sayings.

35. Beware Superfluous Wants and Desires

Moses Maimonides, the great medieval Jewish scholar, doctor and philosopher (1135–1204), left voluminous works behind him and I have not been able to find exactly where this passage comes from. Buddhists speak about attachment producing unhappiness; Christians warn about worldly interests; this warning about superfluous desires is on the same theme. If our wants (as opposed to needs) are many, we are more likely to be unhappy.

36. Today, Take Heaven

A true Renaissance man, Fra Giovanni Giocondo (1433–1515) was a dazzling combination of scholar, engineer and priest. The letter was said to be written to his friend, Countess Allagia Aldobrandeschi on Christmas Eve, 1513. I do not know if this attribution is correct but, even if it is a modern invention, I still think it an inspiration.

37. Be Patterns, Be Examples

The founder of the Society of Friends or Quakers, George Fox (1624–91) travelled round Britain preaching. He was often thrown into prison or driven out of towns. This letter was sent to fellow Quakers in 1656 when Fox was in prison in Launceston, Cornwall. Quakers believe that God or the inner light is in each person. True spirituality is found, not in religious rules, observances, rituals or sacred books but in each person's inner light. Thus we must look for, and cherish, God in our own heart. Rather than making up rules for others, we must set an example for them by our actions.

38. Practical Advice on Changing Your Life for Good

William Penn (1644–1718) was a Quaker, and founder of Pennsylvania. This advice comes out of his book, *The Fruits of Solitude*, published in 1693. Penn was remarkable for the good relationship he had with the native Americans, the Lenni Lenape. Pennsylvania was established on the principle of religious freedom.

39. Nine Spiritual Remedies

I do not know who wrote these. I found them in an old anthology.

40. Twelve Ways to be Happy

I value Robert Louis Stevenson (1850–94) as both a poet and a novelist. I also feel that his poetry is undervalued. I found these twelve suggestions in an anthology and I do not know exactly where they come from, possibly from one of his essays. I can overdo no. 12!

41. The Twelve Steps of Alcoholics Anonymous

These come from what is nicknamed *The Big Book* by AA members, written by Bill Wilson, co-founder of AA (1895–1971) with the help of the early members. The steps are sometimes described as 'spiritual potty training' – an acknowledgment of both their simplicity and their use by people who may previously have led a life devoid of any spiritual or religious meaning. They seem to work to help people recover from all kinds of addiction.

42. Go Placidly Amid the Noise and Haste

Max Ehrmann (1872–1945), a writer, invented these words and launched them on the world, saying that they came off an old tombstone in Baltimore. Their popularity was such that he admitted the invented attribution, and claimed copyright. Some people loathe these words but I like them. While their invented provenance may have helped their acceptance, it is their modernity that makes them mean so much in a fast-moving, hurried society.

43. Make Full Use of This Life

This passage was noted down by one of the disciples of His Divinity Swami Brahmananda Saraswati, Jagadguru, Bhagwan Shankaracharya of Jyotir Math, Himalayas, the spiritual master of His Holiness Maharishi Mahesh Yogi, founder of the world-wide Transcendental Meditation movement. This passage implies a belief in the transmigration of souls after death, but it seems to me it is a powerful thought even to those who do not believe in this.

44. Being True to Self

Ralph Waldo Emerson, writer and poet (1803–82), believed that spiritual renewal thus comes from each person's experience of the 'soul' that permeates creation. We should look within ourselves and within our life, to find spiritual meaning. For this search we need intuitive understanding, not just logic and reason. This passage is about the importance of not just conforming or going along with things, but having the courage of our convictions.

45. Krishna Tells Arjuna how to Work

This is another passage from the 'Bhagavad-Gita', part of India's great epic poem, the *Mahabharata*. It was probably written somewhere between 500 to 200 BC. Gandhi treasured the 'Bhagavad-Gita', seeing it as a guide to daily living. While in prison in the 1920s he wrote pages of commentary on it.

46. The Divinisation of Our Activities

Pierre Teilhard de Chardin (1881–1955) was a startling combination of palaeontologist and Jesuit priest. His book, *The Divine Milieu*, was written in the 1930s but publication was forbidden by his Jesuit order during his lifetime. The book was an attempt to combine scientific thought with Christianity. I am grateful to Peggy Challis who gave it to me to read.

47. Time and Simplicity

Henry David Thoreau, writer and philosopher (1817–62), built himself a log cabin near Walden Pond and lived a natural life for two years, except for a night spent in gaol for failure to pay his poll tax. He put forward the idea of civil disobedience to state authority. His writings were to influence the ecological movement. He argues for simplicity and a different attitude to time – surely important in an age of hurry sickness.

CHAPTER FOUR – LOVING, FORGIVING AND ACCEPTING OTHERS

48. A Definition of Unconditional Love

A hymn to love by St Paul. It needs no commentary by me.

49. Loving Your Neighbour In Judaism

Sometimes Christians behave as if the command to love their neighbour is specifically Christian. This commandment comes in the Old Testament and is part of Judaism. What is more, we must love not just our immediate family, friends, countrymen or co-religionists, but also everyone else. I personally believe that our neighbours include our fellow non-human intelligent beings, the animals.

50. Who Is My Neighbour?

The parable of the good Samaritan is a commentary on, and an extension of, the golden rule in Judaism. Jesus is quoting from Deuteronomy 6:5, and from Leviticus (see 49 above). The point about this story is that Samaritans were heretics. Yet it is the despised outcast, not one of the respectable people, who puts into action the command to love your neighbour as yourself. In this story, outgoing love is more important than religious piety or respectability.

51. Jesus on the Ultimate Proof of Love

This passage from the Gospel of St John puts down the ultimate marker for true altruism – the willingness to die for somebody else. There are individuals who take on huge risks to save other people's lives – fire-fighters, lifeboat rescuers, police, and in some circumstances soldiers. They are willing to risk their lives, not for their friends, but for people they do not even know.

52. Love Your Neighbour in Islam

The *Hadith* are the traditional and authorised stories attributed to the Prophet Muhammad. They make it clear that the emphasis on charitable love is important in Islam. There were women scholars of the *Hadith* who gave and attended lectures.

53. Loving Your Neighbour in Practice

I don't really know where this comes from in John Wesley's many writings, but it is short and clear.

54. The Buddha's Sermon on Returning Good for Evil

This comes from the *Sutra of Forty-Two Sections*, probably the earliest Buddhist scripture to be translated into Chinese soon after 67 AD. Like Jesus Christ's Sermon on the Mount, this sermon by the Buddha specifies returning good for evil.

55. God's Love and Forgiveness

The love of God is boundless, like the love of a good father. It isn't just that the good father takes back the erring son. He does more than that. He gives a feast.

56. Dr Samuel Johnson on Forgiving Early

Samuel Johnson(1709–84), the shambling intellectual and dictionary-maker, is the nearest we have to a Church of England saint. Johnson is best known for his fierce conversation, an area of his life which does not do justice to his kindness. He filled his house with misfits, who sometimes made his life uncomfortable, but they were there because they needed his help. He was also loving to cats and wrote a thundering denunciation of vivisection.

57. Forgiveness Heals Us

Dr Sheila Cassidy was imprisoned in solitary confinement and tortured by the Pinochet regime in Chile in 1975. She has worked for the last 20 years with cancer patients. I found these words on the front cover of the Quaker weekly, *The Friend*. They may have come from one of her books, an article or a talk.

58. A Spirit That Delights to Do No Evil

James Nayler was a Quaker leader. In 1656 he was put on trial for entering Bristol on horseback while his followers spread garments before him and cried out, 'Holy, holy, holy, Lord God of Israel.' He argued that while he was not Christ, Christ was in him. After his release from prison, he set off on foot for home up north but was attacked and robbed on the way. He died from the attack before reaching home. These were his last words.

59. May I Be No Man's Enemy

Eusebius Pamphili, Bishop of Cæsarea in Palestine (b. about 260, d. before 341) is known as the 'father of church history'. During various controversies over theology, Eusebius tried to keep a middle way, and argue for toleration rather than excommunication of heretics – a position which was out of step with the fierce feelings of the time. I hope this prayer is authentic.

60. Of Bearing with the Defects of Others

St Thomas à Kempis (c.1379–1471), formerly known as Thomas Hemerken, was a Christian theologian and a monk and probably the author of *The Imitation of Christ*, from which this passage comes. The book as been described as the most influential work in Christian literature after the Bible. It is worth reading in full.

61. Understanding Others

Mencius or Meng-tse, Chinese philosopher (372–289 BC), believed that with the right education and political system, the innate goodness of human nature could flourish. He travelled from court to court, trying to find a ruler who would put his teaching into practice. Finding none, he retired. This passage was translated by the oriental scholar, Arthur Waley, and read out at his funeral and I am grateful to his stepson who gave it to me. It is a passage which reminds me to pause when passing judgment upon another.

62. A Prayer For Toleration

I have been unable to trace Oliver Warner, who wrote this prayer, which appeared in a Toc H publication. It's a good prayer for our times and a good prayer for Toc H, a community organisation founded in the trenches of World War I by the Rev Tubby Clayton. He set up Talbot House, just behind the Ypres front-line trenches, for rest and recreation. Ahead of its time, it was one of the few places where all ranks, both officers and men, met at the same level. I have made a donation to Toc H in gratitude for this prayer.

63. On Letting Go rather than Controlling

I don't know where these words come from but they are extremely helpful to me. The real love of others only comes when we stop trying to control them. Under the guise of helping I can be very controlling, giving advice or trying to change the behaviour of others, their beliefs, or their circumstances. Under the guise of comforting, I can try to stop people's feelings of grief or pain or anger. This is not love, this is control.

CHAPTER FIVE – DIFFICULTIES, DESPAIR AND GRACE

64. What To Do When in a Difficult Position

When I am perplexed, frightened and under pressure, I often want to lie my way out of trouble or think of some devious method of escape. Thomas Jefferson (1743–1826) says do the right thing and to hell with the consequences! Jefferson was the third president of the United States, principal author of the Declaration of Independence, and an influential politician and philosopher. This passage comes from a letter he wrote to his favourite nephew, Peter Carr.

65. Jesus Talks about Possessions and Anxiety

This reminds us about priorities. We should not worry about our needs, let alone our wants. For me this is a warning about the preoccupying anxiety and obsession which cuts me off from a spiritual life. I suffer from both.

66. Anxiety and Worry Make Things Worse

Francis de Sales (1567–1622), Roman Catholic Bishop of Geneva, is the patron saint of writers. He believed that spiritual perfection is possible for people busy with the affairs of the world and not just those who are in monasteries or convents. This passage comes from one of his letters.

67. The Lord Comforts His People

This passage comes after one about unbelievers who do not listen to God. So the context shows that this is a God who redeems, rather than destroys, sinners.

68. Evils We Inflict on Ourselves

Moses Maimonides (1135–1204) was a Jewish scholar, doctor and philosopher. I don't know where this comes from in his voluminous works. I found it in an anthology. It is difficult to accept that sometimes we play a part in our own unhappiness – easier simply to blame others.

69. Endure Abuse Like the Elephant

The elephant is an emblem of endurance and self-restraint and Buddha himself is called Naga, the Elephant or Mahanaga, the great Elephant. (For more on *The Dhammapada*, see note 32.) There are times when all of us just have to endure. Choosing to endure, rather than having to endure, makes it a little more tolerable. Animals do it and we can perhaps draw inspiration from them.

70. The As If Principle

In despair and unhappiness we somehow have to go on, and sometimes (not always) pretending we feel happier than we are can help us. Occasionally it even switches our mood. This extract comes from 'The Gospel of Relaxation', from *Talks to Teachers on Psychology*, by William James (1842–1910), the US philosopher and psychologist. He was interested in the reality of religious experience and the role of human thinking in the struggle to live happily.

71. On Conquering Melancholy by Active Kindness to Others

This is a good recipe for bad times. But if I take it too far I can become the wounded healer, one of those people whose helping activities may damage others. John Keble (1792–1866) was a theologian and hymn writer. One of the leaders of the Oxford Movement, Keble wanted to revive the high church ideals of Anglicanism. He was best known during his life for *The Christian Year*, a volume of poems for Sundays and church festivals. This comes from one of his letters. I don't have the exact date.

72. Footprints

I know this is a soppy piece of prose but it has helped people in dire times. In deepest depression, I feel that God is absent or, worse, is a God who has contempt and hatred for me. The trick (when I can do it) is to remember that this feeling is an illusion.

73. Daylight

Commentators say that these verses were addressed to the Prophet Muhammad at a time when he was downcast.

74. The Lord Is My Shepherd

This is the Judaic psalm that has become special to Christians, as the image of God as a shepherd is taken up in other places in the New Testament. The staff is the stick with which shepherds drove off dogs and wolves, and the rod is what sheep passed under as they were being counted. Because it is so well known, I have used it as a comfort, saying it over and over again in moments of despair or sorrow.

75. There Is Meaning in Unhappiness

This passage by John Henry Newman, cardinal and writer (1801–90) is very important to me. I don't know where it comes from but I suspect he wrote it during the controversy and pain he suffered when he converted from Anglicanism to Catholicism. When I am very unhappy, I try to remember that the pain may be part of my purpose in life. For instance, my own experience of suicidal depression has helped me sympathise with others going through the same thing.

76. Despair and Recovery from Despair

In *A Confession* and *The Gospel in Brief* by Leo Tolstoy (1828–1910), he describes his journey from despair to faith. The great Russian novelist is best known for his novels, *War and Peace* and *Anna Karenina*. Tolstoy made over his fortune to his wife and tried to live the austere life of a poor peasant. He believed in non-resistance to evil, a doctrine adopted by Gandhi, who corresponded with him. In the conversion experience, darkness leads to light, emotional pain leads to a spiritual insight.

77. Pain, Forgiveness and Letting Go

When I was in despair this book, *Original Blessing* by Matthew Fox, helped me remain a Christian. It is a generous book for all those who feel cast out by or unable to belong to conventional faith. Matthew Fox is president of the new University of Creation Spirituality, 2141 Broadway, Oakland, CA 94612, USA (www.creationspirituality.org). More about him can be found in his autobiography *Confessions: The Making of a Post-Denominational Priest*.

78. Despite Sin All Shall Be Well

From Chapters 27 and 32, *Revelations of Divine Love* by Dame Julian of Norwich (c.1342–c.1413). We know very little about Dame Julian except that she lived in a cell attached to St Julian's church in King Street, Norwich, probably with a window into the church. Her book – which she wrote in English, not Latin – became widely known when Grace Warrack brought out a modernised edition in 1901. What I understand her to say is that sin is a necessary part of redemption, in the same way that fear is necessary for courage.

79. Sin, Separation and Grace

From *The Shaking of the Foundations* by Paul Tillich (1886–1965), theologian and writer. Tillich served as a Lutheran chaplain in the trenches of World War I. He criticised the inadequate traditional conception of God in order to replace it with a better vision. This passage was literally a life-saver for me at a time when I hated myself so much that suicide seemed the correct thing to do, to rid the world of my hateful presence.

CHAPTER SIX – PRAYING AND PRAYERS

80. Prayer Is Like a Lark Soaring Upwards

Jeremy Taylor (1613–67), an Anglican clergyman whose two most famous books are *The Rule and Exercises of Holy Living* (1650) and *The Rule and Exercises of Holy Dying* (1651), was on the king's side during the Civil War. After the restoration of the monarchy he was made a bishop. Though there's a lot I don't warm to within the books, there are passages like this one which are remarkable for their sheer beauty. It comes from one of his sermons.

81. A Non-Religious Understanding of Prayer

This passage from *Honest to God* is an encouragement to pray how we can, not how we can't. I find prayer very difficult indeed and reading this encouraged me to keep trying. It was written in 1963 by the then Bishop of Woolwich, John A. T. Robinson (1919–83), a New Testament scholar and a radical. The book was a popular version of what theologians had been writing for some time. It upset those in the Church who preferred bureaucratic denial of real difficulties in belief.

82. The Practice of the Presence of God

Brother Lawrence (1611–91) was a humble worker in the kitchens. Born Nicholas Herman of Loraine, he was a man of lowly birth who served as a soldier, worked as a footman and then was admitted as a lay brother in a community of Carmelites at Paris in 1666. He took the spiritual name of Brother Lawrence. I have slightly rearranged the text.

83. The Paradox of Prayer

This prayer is said to have been found on the body of an unknown Confederate soldier, during the American Civil War. I have no idea if it is authentic. It may be a modern invention, but it deals with one of the perplexities of spiritual life.

84. Our Father

I have taken this version from the Book of Common Prayer 1662. I like the word 'trespass' better the word 'sin'. It seems to include more – shortcomings, mistakes, failures, as well as deliberate wrongdoing. The word also fits in with the idea of trespassing over emotional boundaries. 'Our Father' packs in most of what we need to say to God.

85. The Prayer of the Sabbath Lights

This prayer comes from *The Jewish Authorised Daily Prayer Book.* The rabbinic authorities in the Middle Ages introduced the practice that at least two special lights should be lit on the eve of the Sabbath. The lights are usually lit by the women of the family and the practice of waving the hands in front of the candles is to summon the spiritual light of the Sabbath into the home. This prayer thus represents the divine in the home. I love the imagery of light and darkness.

86. Eternal Light, Shine into Our Hearts

This lovely prayer was written by Alcuin (732–804), a Yorkshireman and a scholar. He became the headmaster of the York cathedral school until Charlemagne invited him to the school at Aachen and later was abbot of St Martin at Tours. He was a church reformer, a man of holiness but only a deacon, not a priest. I do not know where this prayer is found in his writings.

87. Lord, Make Me a Channel of Thy Peace

One of the best-known prayers of Christianity, written by St Francis of Assisi (1181–1226), the founder of the Franciscan order. He invented the Christmas crib and reminded people to feed the birds in winter. He considered nature to be a mirror of God and called all creatures brothers and sisters. He also helped found a similar order for women, the poor Clares. A man of holy folly and overflowing warmth.

88. St Patrick's Breastplate

This prayer is attributed to St Patrick (c.389–c.461), Irish evangelist. The patron saint of Ireland, he is credited with bringing Christianity to the nation. He wrote a spiritual autobiography. When pagan Saxons invaded the British Isles, it was the Irish who first rechristianised England and saved civilisation. The Celtic model of Christianity, however, was swept aside by the centralised Roman church.

89. Socrates' Prayer

Socrates' prayer comes at the end of *Phaedo*, a dialogue with his young friend Phaedo in which they discuss love and rhetoric. They are walking by a stream and it is when they decide to go back to the city, that Socrates (c. 469–399 BC) suggests offering up a prayer to the deities of the place. The dialogues, like *Phaedo*, in which Socrates is the main protagonist, were written by Plato, the philosopher (c. 427–347 BC), so some people call this Plato's prayer.

90. Slow Me Down, Lord!

Several different people have been credited with writing this prayer. But I first found it with an attribution to Orin L. Crain of the Open Church Foundation and I have made a donation to the church.

91. The Prayer of the Tailor

I found this in a Victorian book about Islam. I have no idea where it comes from, nor if it is at all authentic. This too is about the divinisation of work, finding the spiritual within the material, rather than separate from it.

92. Prayer of Surrender

Iyanla Vanzant is a Christian, a Yoruba priestess, and a TV talk show presenter in the USA. This is a prayer about letting go and forgoing control – my besetting sin. My attempt to control life is a response to my fear. But it is a response which covers up rather than reducing fear. When I can replace fear with trust, I can surrender control.

93. Furnish the Evening with Brightness

Bishop Lancelot Andrewes (1555–1626) was a Church of England theologian who helped produce the Authorised version of the Bible. He refused a bishopric from Queen Elizabeth I but accepted one under James I. He preached in favour of the Church of England's middle way, opposing both Puritanism and Catholicism.

94. Prayers for Fellow Prisoners

The author of this prayer, written on the eve of execution, was Dietrich Bonhoeffer (1906–45), a German Protestant theologian, known for his support of ecumenism and his view of Christianity's role in a secular world. His involvement in the plot to overthrow Adolf Hitler led to his imprisonment and execution. *Prisoner of God: Letters and Papers from Prison* was published posthumously in 1951.

CHAPTER SEVEN – MORTALITY AND DEATH

95. To Everything There is a Time …

This sonorous passage from Ecclesiastes reminds us of the vicissitudes of life. Change is everywhere. Nothing is certain. All life is mutable.

96. The Sparrow in the Hall

Bede's *Ecclesiastical History of the English People* was originally written in Latin, translated into Anglo-Saxon by King Alfred, and then retranslated into English here. Bede was born in 673, became a monk, and died in 735. At a time when books were written by hand he had written, by his own account, 77 volumes by the age of 59. Jesus said that even the fall of a sparrow is important in God's eyes. I think there is an echo here from Matthew 10:29 – 'Are not two sparrows sold for a farthing? and one of them shall not fall on the ground without your Father.'

97. The Death of Socrates

The account of a brave man dying courageously comes in a dialogue in which Phaedo recounts Socrates' last hours in prison. After a discussion about the immortality of the soul, Socrates (c. 469–399 BC) faces death by poison. I find inspiring his choice to meet death willingly, rather than struggle for the last few moments of life. The dialogue, like others in which Socrates talks to his friends, was written by Plato, the philosopher (c.427–347 BC).

98. For Whom the Bell Tolls

John Donne (1572–1631) was a great wit, and a writer of great love poetry, great religious poetry and wonderful sermons. He was finally dean of St Paul's Cathedral, London, where his memorial statue, for which he posed in his shroud, is still to be seen. When Donne fell seriously ill with spotted fever (probably typhus), he used his own life as a source for his writing this book, *The Devotions*. It has 23 sections, charting the course of his sickness and his meditation on it.

99. The Trumpets on the Other Side

John Bunyan (1628–88) was a religious dissident. He joined a separatist church during the Civil War and, with the restoration of the monarchy, was thrown into the county jail for refusing to give an undertaking not to hold a nonconformist service. While in jail – for 12 years – he published his spiritual autobiography and probably started writing *Pilgrim's Progress* – possibly the most-read Christian book after the Bible.

100. A Prayer for the Dead

John Henry Newman (1801–90) was an Anglican clergyman in the Oxford Movement who converted to Catholicism – a choice that in those days meant considerable social and financial trouble. This passage, from *The Dream of Gerontius*, was a poetic version of the then Latin Catholic requiem offices. Newman also wrote such well-known hymns as 'Praise to the holiest in the height' and 'Firmly I believe and truly'.